CW01511984

THE INTELLIGENT SPY'S HANDBOOK

SPIES AND WRITERS, WRITERS AND SPIES
AND THE CONTRIBUTION OF BRITISH
SPIES TO ENGLISH LITERATURE

THE

INTELLIGENT

SPY'S

HANDBOOK

———

ROBIN RENWICK

Biteback Publishing

First published in Great Britain in 2024 by
Biteback Publishing Ltd, London
Copyright © Robin Renwick 2024

ISBN 978-1-78590-902-3

10 9 8 7 6 5 4 3 2 1

A CIP catalogue record for this book is available from the British Library.

Set in Adobe Caslon Pro and Gill Sans MT Pro

Printed and bound in Great Britain by
CPI Group (UK) Ltd, Croydon CR0 4YY

'We have been fortunate to have enjoyed the
services of some very interesting spies.'
MAURICE OLDFIELD, MI6

'I was brought up on Kim.'
HAROLD 'KIM' PHILBY

CONTENTS

INTRODUCTION

This book begins with the story of the supposedly infamous Francis Walsingham, celebrated by Edmund Spenser in 'The Faerie Queene' but with a dire reputation since, and of the genuinely infamous Sir George Downing, creator of Downing Street, described by his deputy, Samuel Pepys, as an utter villain. It is a story of spies turning into writers and of writers and poets, including John Milton, moonlighting as spies and of the relationships between them.

The first of all great spy storytellers, Rudyard Kipling, published *Kim* in 1900. Erskine Childers wrote his bestseller, the 1903 novel *The Riddle of the Sands*, to alert his readers to the danger of a German invasion, only then to turn into a traitor who was executed not by the British but by the Free Irish government. Other notable employees of the intelligence branches of the British government were the poets and playwrights Christopher Marlowe and Andrew Marvell, Cromwell's other spymaster, John Thurloe, and Wellington's code breaker, George Scovell.

Thereafter, you will encounter a leading practitioner of the 'Great Game' against the Russians in Central Asia who became *The Spy Who Disappeared*, while a Colonel Bailey got himself hired by the Bolshevik secret police to hunt for an anti-Bolshevik Englishman, in fact himself.

There followed T. E. Lawrence, who achieved far more than most but romanticised a lot about it; Compton Mackenzie, who favoured poisoning the pro-German King of Greece; Sidney Reilly, the so called 'ace of spies', who came to a sticky end plotting against the Bolsheviks; the code breaker Admiral 'Blinker' Hall; Mansfield Cumming, the first 'C'; Somerset Maugham, William Stephenson, who employed the code name 'Intrepid'; the very professional Fitzroy Maclean and Ian Fleming; rank amateurs like Malcolm Muggeridge and Graham Greene; and, most courageous of all, Oleg Gordievsky. Was Arthur Ransome a Bolshevik agent? If he wasn't, his wife Evgenia Shelepina (Trotsky's secretary) certainly was.

Greene was so obsessed by espionage that four of his novels were about it. But why did he side with Philby? And why did so many of his former colleagues in MI6 dislike the works of John le Carré? And how did Ian Fleming create a hero, based on himself, whose exploits proved capable of attracting seven billion viewings?

Other features of this story are a couple of *femmes fatales* – Catherine Walston (for Graham Greene) and Ann Rothermere (for Ian Fleming). It is hard to think of a more extraordinary cast of characters.

The intelligent spy will wish to know something about the adventures of his or her illustrious predecessors, factual or fictional, given, as this will show, the frequent crossovers between the two.

Who can doubt, for instance, that Ian Fleming's SMERSH is functioning in Putin's Russia and beyond today?

Any book about our latter day spy/writers must pay homage to their biographers: Norman Sherry for Graham Greene; John Pearson, Andrew Lycett and Nicholas Shakespeare for Ian Fleming; and Adam Sisman for John le Carré; also to the most distinguished historian of Britain's intelligence services, Christopher Andrew.

Members of the British Foreign Service were and are trained to refer to their colleagues in the intelligence services as 'Our Friends'. In the course of my diplomatic career, I received a lot of help from them; hence this book in their honour.

CHAPTER I

WALSINGHAM

The first British spy to exercise a hypnotic fascination over the public and writers of his time, as well as on his appalled opponents in Spain and France, was the most ruthless and successful British spymaster of them all.

Francis Walsingham was born in 1532 on the estate near Chislehurst in Kent of a prominent and very well connected family. One uncle was Lieutenant of the Tower of London; another became Chancellor of the Exchequer. He studied law at Cambridge before travelling in Europe then returning to continue his studies at Gray's Inn. A devout Protestant, he left Britain to join other English Protestant expatriates in Switzerland when the Catholic Queen Mary succeeded her brother, Edward VI, in 1553. The Archbishop of Canterbury, Thomas Cranmer, and other Protestant notables accused of treason were burnt at the stake, and Protestants were further horrified when Mary married the future King Philip II of Spain.

Walsingham returned to serve the new Queen as soon as the Protestant Elizabeth succeeded Mary, her half-sister, when she died in 1558. He was elected to Parliament in the following year. He became active in gathering support for the Huguenots (Protestants) in France. By 1569, he was working with William Cecil to counter Catholic plots against Elizabeth.

In that year, the 'Northern Rebellion' was led by the Catholic Earls of Westmoreland and Northumberland, seeking to depose Elizabeth and replace her with the Catholic Mary, Queen of Scots, who had been ousted from her monarchy in Scotland and had sought refuge under Elizabeth's protection (and surveillance) in England. The rebels were defeated north of York. Northumberland was executed; Westmoreland fled abroad.

Walsingham's first success was in uncovering the Ridolfi plot to organise a ten thousand man invasion of Britain to be led by the Spanish commander in the Netherlands and join forces with Catholic members of the nobility to kill Elizabeth and replace her with Mary, Queen of Scots. The torture of suspected conspirators was standard operating procedure at the time, questioned by no one in authority in England, France or Spain. Ridolfi, who confessed to being a papal spy, was interrogated at Walsingham's house. The Duke of Norfolk, implicated in the plot, was executed. The Spanish Ambassador was expelled. Philip II of Spain supported the plot, as did Mary, increasing Elizabeth's suspicions about her.

In 1570, Walsingham was appointed Ambassador to France to support the Huguenots in their negotiations with King Charles IX. He also was supposed to continue negotiations for a possible marriage between Elizabeth and Charles's younger brother, the Duke of Anjou. The plan was dropped because of Anjou's Catholicism. An alternative match was proposed with Charles's younger brother, but Walsingham reported him as being ugly and 'void of a good humour'. Walsingham was against the whole idea of a French marriage for the Queen and worked instead for a defensive military alliance with France against Spain, which was concluded in the Treaty of Blois in 1572.

Walsingham had formed close friendships with the prominent Huguenot families in Paris at the time. The Huguenots were supporting the revolt of their fellow Protestants in the Spanish controlled Netherlands. On the night of 24–25 August 1572, the regime of King Charles IX and Catherine de' Medici unleashed the St Bartholomew's Day massacre against all the leading Huguenots. They were attacked by the Paris mob and subjected to targeted assassinations. Gaspard de Coligny, the military and political leader of the Huguenots, and the other prominent Huguenots were hunted down and killed. Over the next several weeks, the massacre was extended to the countryside and other towns.

Walsingham found himself powerless to save Huguenot friends, who appealed to him for help. The poet and courtier, Sir Philip Sidney, who also opposed a French marriage, was able to seek refuge in his embassy (he later married Walsingham's daughter). Several Huguenots were killed as they tried to do so. Walsingham never forgot the scenes he witnessed then. The experience embedded in him an enmity to Catholics for the rest of his life and a determination to stop at nothing to protect his Queen from further Catholic plots against her.

Nor were his fears on that score unfounded. For although Elizabeth had sponsored a religious settlement under which Catholics were permitted to worship privately, in February 1570 Pope Pius

V issued the bull *Regnans in Excelsis* excommunicating Elizabeth, effectively putting a price on her head and purportedly depriving her of sovereignty over England and Ireland. The Pope and the Spanish government had been outraged by English support for the Protestant rebellion in the Netherlands, of which Walsingham was a strong advocate.

Walsingham returned to London in 1573. He was appointed joint principal secretary, a position that became that of Secretary of State. Walsingham's close associations were with the new merchant class rather than with the nobility, many of whom were still Catholics. He was a strong supporter of their overseas ventures, including Francis Drake's circumnavigation of the globe, at the conclusion of which the Queen dined with and knighted him on his ship.

Drake was given a privateer's commission by the Queen, allowing him and his cousin, John Hawkins, to attack Spanish targets, mainly in the West Indies, as they wished. When the Spanish Ambassador was granted an audience with Elizabeth, he was outraged to see her wearing a necklace looted by Drake or Hawkins from a Spanish treasure ship. The great historian of English exploration worldwide, Richard Hakluyt, dedicated his first work to Walsingham.

Walsingham advocated direct intervention in support of the Protestant revolt in the Netherlands, but his fellow Secretary of State, William Cecil, was more cautious, advocating an attempt at mediation, which Elizabeth supported. William Cecil, later Lord Burghley, was by nature more conciliatory than Walsingham and the founding member of the great Cecil dynasty, members of which held senior positions in successive British governments for the next three centuries. But he agreed with Walsingham about the potentially mortal danger posed to the Queen by Mary, Queen of Scots.

When Charles IX died in France and was succeeded by his brother Henry III, the idea was revived of a match between the Queen and the younger brother, the Duke of Anjou, who was portraying himself as a protector of the Protestants and a potential leader for the Dutch.

In 1581, Walsingham was sent to Paris to pursue this and the possibility of an alliance with the French. But the French wanted first a marriage, then an alliance. Walsingham insisted on an alliance first and returned to London without an agreement. He remained as opposed as ever to the marriage, as Anjou was a Catholic and likely heir to the French throne. As Elizabeth was childless, such a marriage could end up with the French monarchy in control.

Walsingham compared the proposed marriage to that between the Protestant Henry of Navarre and the Catholic Margaret of Valois, which had contributed to triggering the St Bartholomew massacre, 'the most horrible spectacle' he had ever witnessed. He suggested that similar riots might happen in Britain if it went ahead. Elizabeth did not seem to mind his uncompromising advice, describing him in a letter to him as 'her Moor [who] cannot change his colour!'

Tensions continued over policy towards France, with Walsingham distrustful of the English Ambassador, Edward Stafford, who he suspected of being in the pay of Spain, as indeed he was, due to his gambling debts. Walsingham accordingly fed disinformation to Stafford for him to pass on to Madrid.

In 1578, the pro-English Regent of Scotland, who Walsingham supported, was overthrown. Walsingham was sent to Scotland on a mission he did not expect to succeed and it didn't. Mary's son, James VI, in whose favour she had been obliged to abdicate, told

Walsingham that he was an 'absolute King' in Scotland. Walsingham's response was that 'young princes [are] carried into great errors upon an opinion of the absoluteness of their royal authority and do not consider that when they transgress the bounds and limits of the law, they leave to be kings and become tyrants'. A mutual defence pact with Scotland later was agreed in the 1586 Treaty of Berwick.

The fate of the Protestants in France was ever present in Walsingham's mind. He tracked down proselytising Catholic priests and supposed conspirators by employing informers and intercepting correspondence. His staff included the cryptographer, Thomas Phelippes, who was an expert in forgery and deciphering letters. Another staffer, Arthur Gregory, was an expert at breaking and re-constituting seals without detection. Edmund Campion was among those tortured, found guilty of conspiracy and publicly executed at Tyburn.

In 1582, letters from the Spanish Ambassador to contacts in Scotland were intercepted, revealing further plans for the Catholic powers to invade England and replace Elizabeth by Mary, Queen of Scots. Walsingham installed a spy in the French Embassy in London. Francis Throckmorton confessed under torture to being involved in this conspiracy. He was executed and another Spanish Ambassador was expelled. These activities led to regular hostile mentions of Walsingham in Mary's decoded messages.

By 1584, England was militarily involved in supporting the Protestant revolt in the Netherlands. The assassination of the Protestant leader, William the Silent, increased fears that a similar attempt might be made to kill Elizabeth. Walsingham and Cecil, by now Lord Burghley, drew up the Bond of Association, committing all the signatories to executing anyone who attempted to usurp the throne or to assassinate the Queen. Mary herself was required to sign this document. She was placed in the strict custody of Sir Amias Paulet, a friend of Walsingham, in a moated manor house at Chartley, near Stafford. All her correspondence was to be opened. But Walsingham set a deliberate trap for Mary, who was led to believe that messages sent via a beer keg were secure.

In 1586, Anthony Babington wrote to Mary about a plot to free her and kill Elizabeth. Six noble gentlemen were pledged to kill Elizabeth. When Thomas Phelippes decoded Mary's reply, he drew on it the portrait of a gallows. For Mary encouraged Babington, when the time was right, to 'sett the six gentlemen to work'. Babington and his associates were rounded up and executed. Mary was put on trial by thirty-six commissioners, including Walsingham. During the trial, Mary pointed at Walsingham and said, 'All of this is the work of Monsieur de Walsingham for my destruction.' He replied that, as Secretary of State, he had done nothing but his duty.

She was found guilty and the warrant for her execution was drafted, but Elizabeth was reluctant to sign it, despite the urgings of Walsingham, who then wrote to Sir Amias Paulet urging him to find 'some way to shorten the life' of Mary to relieve the Queen of that burden, to which Paulet sent a splendid reply: 'God forbid that I should make so foul a shipwreck of my conscience, or leave so great a blot to my poor posterity, to shed blood without law or warrant.'

Walsingham pressed ahead with plans to execute Mary. On 1 February 1587, Elizabeth signed the warrant for the execution, entrusting it to the junior Secretary of State, William Davison.

Davison passed the warrant to Cecil and a Privy Council convened by Cecil without informing the Queen agreed to carry out the sentence as soon as possible. Mary was beheaded shortly afterwards.

On hearing of the execution, Elizabeth claimed not to have sanctioned it and that the warrant should not have been passed on by Davison, who was imprisoned for over a year in the Tower. Walsingham was not at court in the weeks preceding the execution and appeared to suffer no signs of the Queen's displeasure. In reality, she must by then have been glad to have this threat removed and to have had enough of Mary's plotting.

King Philip II of Spain was outraged by England's continuing support to the Protestant revolt against Spanish rule in the Netherlands and the attacks on Spanish settlements and ships in the Caribbean. Spain at the time, with its vast empire, was a far more important power than England, which did not yet have one. The French writer Exquemelin described the British privateers as descending on peaceful Spanish settlements in the Caribbean like wolves, terrorising the population, seizing valuables and looting churches.

From 1586, Walsingham had been receiving numerous reports from his agents in Europe in the merchant communities and foreign governments about Spanish plans for an invasion of England. A key source for him was Anthony Standen, a friend of the Tuscan Ambassador to Madrid, who was in the confidence of the Spanish government. Standen's despatches to Walsingham were very revealing about Spanish intentions. In response, Walsingham personally supervised the reinforcement of Dover harbour. Through the British Ambassador in Turkey, he tried unsuccessfully to persuade the

Ottoman regime to attack Spain in the Mediterranean. More to the point, he kept in close touch with Spanish naval preparations.

In 1587, the intelligence about these showed the Spaniards concentrating a massive fleet in Cádiz for an attempted invasion of England. Walsingham was part architect of Sir Francis Drake's attack on the Spanish fleet in its harbour, which Drake described as 'singeing the King of Spain's beard'. The attack frustrated Spanish plans until the following year.

The 130 ship Armada for the invasion of Britain, despatched by King Philip II of Spain, sailed from Lisbon at the end of May 1588, commanded by the Duke of Medina Sidonia, who had no previous naval experience. His instructions were to sail through the English Channel to link up with the Spanish forces in the Netherlands and escort an invasion force to overthrow Elizabeth and reinstate Catholicism in England, ending English support for the Dutch Republic and the attacks by English privateers on Spanish interests in the Americas.

Based in Plymouth, Drake had plenty of warning of the approach of the Spanish fleet, though the tale of him insisting on finishing his game of bowls was apocryphal. The Spanish fleet was attacked by faster and more manoeuvrable English ships throughout its passage through the Channel. On reaching Calais, it was attacked by Drake and Hawkins with fireships. In the ensuing battle of Gravelines, off the Dutch coast, it suffered heavy losses, with the surviving vessels obliged to escape into the North Sea and then to try to return to Spain around the north of Scotland and through the Irish Sea.

In her speech to the Earl of Dudley's anti-invasion troops at Tilbury on 9 August 1588, Elizabeth was reported to have said, 'We have been persuaded by some that are careful of our security [no doubt Cecil and Walsingham] to take heed how we commit ourselves to armed multitudes, for fear of treachery.' But she did not distrust her loving people. 'Let tyrants fear … I know I have the body of a weak and feeble woman, but I have the heart and stomach of a King.'

On 18 August, following the dispersal of the Armada, the naval commander Lord Henry Seymour wrote to Walsingham, 'You have fought more with your pen than many have in our English navy fought with their enemies.'

Walsingham died on 6 April 1590. He had received from his Queen a tablet engraved 'An Allegory of the Tudor Succession' inscribed:

> The Queen to Walsingham this tablet sent
> Mark of her people's and her own content

Walsingham did not need to become a legend; he was one in his own lifetime. He was revered and celebrated by the leading Protestant writers and poets of his time, including his son in law, Philip Sidney. Edmund Spenser included a sonnet to Walsingham in his epic poem in honour of Elizabeth, 'The Faerie Queene'. Sir John Davies and Thomas Watson, fellow Protestants, wrote eulogies about him, while the Jesuit Robert Persons denounced his persecution of Catholics as cruel and inhumane.

In his last novel, *A Dead Man in Deptford*, Anthony Burgess revived conspiracy theories about Walsingham, including his supposed involvement in the death of the playwright Christopher Marlowe, who had been a spy but was killed in a tavern brawl after Walsingham's death. The 1998 film *Elizabeth*, with a brilliant performance as Walsingham by Geoffrey Rush, portrayed him as irreligious, whereas he was a committed Protestant, as sexually ambiguous, for which no evidence exists, and as responsible for the murder of Mary of Guise, which he wasn't. He featured also in *Elizabeth: The Golden Age* and in quite recent BBC and Channel Four series, generally as a dark and malevolent figure.

Inevitably, biographers of Mary, Queen of Scots have tended to disregard the evidence that she brought her disasters on herself. It was not Walsingham who got her dethroned in Scotland. Having married the questionable Lord Darnley, who plotted against her, she saw her Private Secretary David Rizzio stabbed to death, by a group including Darnley, in front of her. Darnley then was killed when his lodgings were destroyed by gunpowder; though he appeared to have been strangled, not blown up. The explosion was blamed on her next husband, to whom she may have been married forcibly, the Earl of Bothwell. The 'casket letters', attributed to Mary, purported to show an adulterous relationship with Bothwell before Darnley was killed.

Following an uprising by the Scottish nobles against the couple, Mary was forced to abdicate in favour of her infant son, James VI. Having sought refuge in England, she was kept under surveillance in a series of castles and large houses but was allowed a substantial retinue, until plots relating to her started to be organised against Elizabeth. She did not have the wit to understand that her chances of survival depended on her discouraging plots against her cousin and captor, rather than encouraging them as, undoubtedly, she proceeded then to do. Walsingham and Cecil had good reason to regard her as a threat to the Queen.

Nevertheless, it was extraordinary for the chief spymaster to occupy a position of such power and influence in the state. Spies thereafter in Britain could expect to enjoy only far more humble roles and never really came back into such favour until more modern times.

Unlike his counterpart, William Cecil, Walsingham left no grand house or dynasty behind. Walsingham's daughter, Frances, married the poet, scholar and soldier Philip Sidney. When Sidney was killed fighting courageously in the Netherlands, Walsingham paid for a funeral so grand that it nearly bankrupted him. He died owing the Crown the same amount of money as the Crown owed him.

Frances then married Robert Devereux, the second Earl of Essex, who was a cousin of Elizabeth. Having been for a while the Queen's favourite, his conduct became so outrageous that she concluded that he was 'not of a nature to be ruled'. Having at first enjoyed some military success, after a failed command in Ireland, he attempted to seize power by organising a small rebellion in London that was easily suppressed, following which he was executed.

CHAPTER II

CROMWELL'S SPIES

The Stuart monarchs who succeeded Elizabeth, except for Charles II, paid little heed to Walsingham's warning to the youthful James VI not to imagine that they had absolute power, resulting in the execution of Charles I and the ousting of James II.

Walsingham had no successors worthy of the name. But Cromwell was supported by two spymasters: John Thurloe and George Downing. Assisting them as Secretary of the Department of Foreign Tongues was the ardently republican poet John Milton, a talented linguist who, despite going blind, served in that position throughout the Cromwellian regime. Serving as one of his deputies was another poet, Andrew Marvell.

Milton was not much of a spy, being more of a polemicist. The blood had scarcely dried from the beheading of Charles I when he published a pamphlet justifying the regicide. His appointment as head of the bureau was a reward for Milton acting as the main propagandist for the regime, responding, for instance 'in defence of the English people' to a bestselling Royalist account of Charles I's purported thoughts in his last days. He started one of his sonnets with the words 'Cromwell, our chief of men'.

John Thurloe was a lawyer who had no involvement in the execution of Charles I, declaring that he 'was altogether stranger to that fact, and to all the counsels about it'. But he was a supporter of Cromwell and was appointed as his Secretary of State in 1652. He became his head of intelligence and ran a network of agents in Europe and at home. He employed the revered mathematician John Wallis, who established a code breaking department. It was said of Wallis that he had no strong convictions; what motivated him was 'sheer enjoyment in the art and ingenuity' required to break codes.

Thurloe's department broke up the 'Sealed Knot', a secret society of Royalists, and uncovered various other plots against Cromwell's Protectorate. He made huge efforts to intercept communications with Charles II in exile and to find or plant an agent in his court there. In 1655, he became Postmaster General, consolidating his ability to intercept correspondence. He exposed Edward Sexby's 1657 plot to assassinate Cromwell. He failed at first to act against another would be assassin, having received 'so many advertisements' of the kind, but he did then arrest Miles Sindercombe and his accomplices in time to forestall another attempt against Cromwell.

He was described as being 'so much in all Cromwell's secrets' that it was very unsafe to attack him. Having 'turned' a member of the Sealed Knot, Sir Richard Willis, in concert with Richard Cromwell, Thurloe then devised a plan to decapitate the Royalists by trying to get Willis to lure the future King and his brothers, the Dukes of York and Gloucester, then in exile in Flanders, to attempt a landing in Sussex, supposedly to be greeted by Royalist supporters, when the intention was in fact to shoot them.

His deputy, Samuel Morland, by then ready to change sides, warned Charles's entourage against this. Following the Restoration, in May 1660, Thurloe was charged with high treason but then released. He featured as a character in the play *Cromwell* by Victor Hugo and captured the imagination of many historical novelists, including Robert Wilton in *Traitor's Field* and BBC television producers in their series *By the Sword Divided*.

Cromwell's other spymaster, George Downing, was born in Ireland around 1623. He was a nephew of John Winthrop, Governor of Massachusetts. His father was a barrister and a Puritan. They moved to Salem in Massachusetts for a while in 1638. He graduated from Harvard in the first graduating class there in 1642. He then returned to England, becoming initially a chaplain in the regiment of one of Cromwell's lieutenants, Colonel John Okey, who, reportedly, had sponsored his education. An ardent republican, he supported the execution in January 1649 of Charles I and then participated in the battles of Dunbar and Worcester. He was appointed Scoutmaster General of Cromwell's forces in Scotland, in charge of collecting intelligence and managing a network of spies, then as a Teller of the Exchequer. In 1657, he was appointed Ambassador to the Dutch Republic.

As ambassador, he concentrated on intelligence gathering about Dutch intentions and Royalist plots. He kept his post during the political turmoil that followed the downfall of Cromwell's heir, Richard, in a period in which a wit produced the following epigram:

> Treason never Prospers
> What's the Reason?
> If it doth Prosper
> None dare call it Treason

George Downing solved the problem of turning his coat and reconciling with the future Charles II by leaking to him the despatches of his fellow Cromwellian spy, John Thurloe, including his plot to decapitate the Royalists. Downing declared that he had been misled by ideas 'sucked in' while he was in New England, of which he now 'saw the error'. So, on the Restoration of Charles II, he was knighted and confirmed in his post, as well as being granted an area of land near St James's Park, on which later he proceeded to build the present day Downing Street.

Under the Restoration, he organised spy rings to hunt down many of his former colleagues. He arranged the arrest in Holland of the regicides John Barkstead and Miles Corbet and of his former commander and sponsor, John Okey. Against Dutch protests, they were taken to London and executed. Samuel Pepys, though admitting that his conduct was 'useful to the King', described him as 'a perfidious rogue', adding that 'all the world took notice of him for a most ungrateful villain for his pains'.

In March 1665, the increasing mercantile rivalry with the Netherlands and the seizure of Dutch ships precipitated the Second Anglo-Dutch War. The war party in London was led by the future James II. Downing, who kept predicting that the Dutch would give way and even tried to engineer a coup against their leader, Johan de Witt, was expelled from the Netherlands for espionage. He was more successful in advocating the seizure from the Dutch of their colony of New Amsterdam, the present day New York. To this day, two streets in New York are named after him.

The war turned into a disaster. In June 1667, Samuel Pepys, administrator of the Royal Navy, lamented in his diary the lack of intelligence about and preparation against the successful Dutch attack on

English warships in the Thames and Medway, when many of them were set on fire while still at anchor. This was acknowledged at the time to have been 'the most serious defeat the Royal Navy has ever had in its home waters'.

On returning to the Netherlands in 1671, Downing was chased out of the country by an enraged mob. Having secured the piece of land he coveted, adjoining St James's Park, existing houses on the site were pulled down and he employed Sir Christopher Wren to build houses along the north side of the cul-de-sac. To maximise profit, the houses were built with poor foundations on the marshy ground. Winston Churchill wrote of Downing Street that No. 10 and the other houses there were 'shaky and lightly built by the prof- iteering contractor whose name they bear'.

King George II presented the Downing Street house and one immediately behind it, overlooking the Horse Guards, to Sir Robert Walpole, who declined it as a gift but asked that it should be made available to him and his successors as First Lords of the Treasury, the title that became that of Prime Minister. Once the two houses had been joined together, Walpole took up residence there in 1735.

The United Kingdom always claims not to have been successfully invaded since 1066. But on 5 November 1688, William of Orange, who had married Mary Stuart, niece of Charles II, landed with a Dutch army at Brixham in Devon. His fleet of 450 ships was far larger than the Spanish Armada and he landed with forty thousand men. He had, it was true, been formally invited to do so in a letter delivered to him in June by the 'Immortal Seven' Protestant leaders (six nobles and one Bishop) to save the country from the Catholic James II. The self appointed Seven had written that they had 'great reason to believe, we shall be every day in a worse condition ...

there are nineteen parts out of twenty of the people throughout the kingdom who are desirous of a change' and who would willingly contribute to it if they had protection in their rising.

So this change of regime was less of a conspiracy than most, except that, before launching his invasion, William secured an assurance from James's ablest commander, Lord Churchill of Eyemouth, that he was a Protestant and 'you have but to command me'. William declared on landing that he had done so to protect Protestantism and the liberties of England, and Churchill encouraged Protestant army officers to defect to him. In camp, still nominally on James's side, on 24 November Churchill slipped away with four hundred officers and men, effectively ending resistance to William. He wrote to James II that he was 'actuated by a higher principle'. Churchill was rewarded by being made Earl, later Duke of Marlborough.

CHAPTER III

THE ABSENCE OF
ORGANISED INTELLIGENCE

Throughout the eighteenth century, there was no formal intelligence organisation at the Admiralty. Intelligence was supplied in reports from British diplomatic missions, including that of Sir William Hamilton in Naples, the complaisant husband of Nelson's mistress, Emma, who served in the post for thirty-six years. Through the Post Office, the authorities could intercept correspondence, including opening diplomatic pouches. Captured code books were another source. But it could take weeks or even months to transfer information to commanders at sea. Nelson's ships could signal to each other and to shore installations but no further than that. So Nelson had to rely above all on his frigates for information, constantly complaining that he never had enough of them.

A more serious effort to collect intelligence was made from 1782 by the former naval officer and Under Secretary at the Home Office Evan Nepean, who then served at the Admiralty until 1804. He paid for a network of spies to cover French naval activity at Toulon, Brest and along the Normandy coast. Nepean's agents included Richard Etches, who originally spied for Catherine the Great before changing sides, with a detailed knowledge of the North Sea and Baltic countries. In 1798, Etches helped Sir Sidney Smith to escape from the Temple prison in Paris.

But Nelson missed the departure of Napoleon with the French fleet from Toulon and neither he nor the tiny staff at the Admiralty had any clear idea where it was heading – an episode that triggered the first documented inquiry into an intelligence failure. Nelson's pursuit of it took three months before he finally found and destroyed the fleet in the battle of Aboukir Bay. Before Trafalgar, he chased the French fleet to the West Indies and back without ever making contact with it.

His frigates, however, were able to observe the huge French and Spanish fleet at anchor in Cádiz before it ventured out on 18 October 1805. Though Nelson had fewer ships, Admiral Villeneuve was not keen to risk his fleet, warning Napoleon that Nelson was not a normal adversary and might destroy them all. But with his *Grande Armée* ready to invade Britain, Napoleon insisted that Villeneuve must sail out to fight and sent another Admiral to replace him if he didn't.

The exception to the norm throughout this long period of British naval and military commanders operating with no formal or organised intelligence gathering was the Duke of Wellington. In the Peninsula War against the French in Portugal, then Spain, Wellington did have an intelligence organisation and could count on a vast amount of information on French troop movements supplied to him by his Portuguese and then Spanish allies. He deployed his own 'exploring' reconnaissance officers and guides, and in Colonel (later General) George Scovell, he had an extremely gifted linguist. Scovell assembled a polyglot group of diverse nationalities recruited for their local knowledge and language skills called the Army Guides. They developed a system for intercepting and deciphering French communications.

In 1811, the French began using a code based on 150 numbers known as the Army of Portugal code. Scovell cracked the code within two days. At the end of the year, a new code called the Great Paris Code was sent to all French Army officers. This was based on 1,400 numbers and on an earlier French diplomatic code (the *Grand Chiffre*). By December 1812, when a letter from his brother, Joseph Bonaparte, installed as King of Spain, to Napoleon was intercepted, Scovell was able to decipher enough of his account of French operations and plans to make a vital contribution to Wellington's victory in the battle of Vitoria in June 1813.

In 1815, however, Wellington had no foreknowledge of Napoleon's rapid crossing of the Belgian border to attack him at Waterloo, which he heard of only when attending the Duchess of Richmond's ball. Nor did he have any rapid means of communicating with his Prussian ally, Marshal Blucher, whose forces only arrived very late in the day at Waterloo.

CHAPTER IV

THE GREAT GAME

The Great Game, the subject of an excellent book by Peter Hopkirk, was the espionage cum exploration story of the rivalry between Britain and Russia for supremacy in Central Asia from the mid nineteenth century. The British had no desire to extend their empire into the dirt poor, inaccessible and ungovernable terrain of Afghanistan, but did not want the Russians there either, or dominant elsewhere in the region. To some extent, the British fears were exaggerated, as neither Tsars nor Bolsheviks had the capacity to directly threaten India. But they did seek domination over Central Asia and, if possible, Afghanistan.

The term itself was coined by Captain Arthur Conolly of the Bengal Light Cavalry in the employ of the East India Company. In 1840, he wrote to Henry Rawlinson, who had been appointed as the political agent in Kandahar, about the 'grand game' that lay in front of them. Often travelling in disguise, he used 'Khan Ali' as his pseudonym. A journey from Moscow to India via Herat in 1830–31 established his reputation as a travel writer. In 1841, to counter increasing Russian penetration of Central Asia, he tried unsuccessfully to persuade the various khanates to settle their differences. In Bukhara, he was captured on a mission to try to rescue a Colonel Stoddart, who had preceded him there. Both were charged with spying for the British Empire and beheaded in the main square of Bukhara by the Emir, Nasrullah Khan.

For decades thereafter, a series of other outstandingly brave and resourceful young officers were despatched from India, with little support and often in disguises that very rarely can have fooled the locals, to discover what was happening far beyond the North West Frontier with Afghanistan. Favoured roles included travelling as monks or as horse traders. Their key tasks were to discover which of the local khans were friendly or irredeemably hostile and to detect any sign of the Russians coming in the opposite direction, as they engaged in their own version of the Great Game. Apart from serving as the eyes and ears of the empire, it was far from clear what some of these isolated and extremely risky missions were intended to achieve, but Victorian England was proud of the courage of those who undertook them, devouring enthusiastically the accounts they published of their adventures.

The First Anglo-Afghan War (1839–42) was triggered when the Russians sent an envoy, Count Witkiewicz, to persuade Dost Mohammed Khan, the ruler of Kabul, to form an alliance against the British. This panicked the British Governor General of India, Lord Auckland, into launching an invasion, condemned by the Duke of Wellington as 'stupid', as Afghanistan was a land of 'rocks, sands, deserts, ice and snow'. He forecast that the invaders would easily defeat the tribal forces, only then to find themselves struggling to hold on.

The war ended in disaster for the British, as the undersized garrison left behind with numerous camp followers were massacred as they tried to withdraw. Dr William Brydon, galloping into the fort at Jalalabad with Afghans in hot pursuit, was inaccurately described as the only British officer to survive, though most of the others didn't. In 1842, a punitive expedition was launched to destroy Kabul, whereupon the British withdrew. From 1865, the Russians embarked on a far more determined forward policy in Central Asia, annexing first Tashkent, then Samarkand and Bukhara.

Colonel Fred Burnaby was a massive, twenty stone cavalry and intelligence officer who spoke several languages. In 1875, in a moment of *détente* with Tsarist Russia, he travelled to Central Asia, initially with the agreement of the Russians, though then encountering difficulties with them. His account of his adventures in *A Ride to Khiva* was an early bestselling adventure story, for which he was lionised in London society.

Within two years, a Russian proponent of the Great Game, Colonel Grodekov, was planning a road from Tashkent to Herat via Samarkand, which Burnaby saw as a clear threat to India. After more adventures, including crossing the Channel in a balloon, Burnaby was killed in hand to hand fighting against the Dervishes on the Upper Nile.

In 1878, to forestall Russian ambitions in that direction, the British launched a fresh invasion of Afghanistan, defeating the Amir, Sher Ali Khan. A treaty was signed, but a British mission to Kabul then was massacred, triggering a second invasion, led by Lord Roberts, and the installation of a new Amir willing to work with the British, following which Roberts, very sensibly, withdrew.

In 1889, Francis Younghusband, the future British resident in

Kashmir, encountered a leading Russian practitioner of the Great Game, Colonel, later General, Grombchevsky, with a contingent of Cossacks on the border of Ladakh. They dined together, with lashings of vodka and brandy. The Cossacks displayed their horsemanship; Younghusband's Gurkhas showed off their rifle skills. The British denied the Russians entry to Ladakh.

Two years later, in the desolate Pamir mountains north of Kashmir, Younghusband was annoyed to be ordered away by another bunch of Cossacks under Colonel Yonov, planting a Tsarist flag. Younghusband's tales of his adventures, especially *The Heart of a Continent*, were devoured by Victorian readers in Britain.

In 1893, the Durand Line Agreement was signed with the Afghans, fixing the territorial limits of each side. It has never been accepted by the Afghan Taliban, as it leaves some Pashtun tribes on what is now the Pakistan side of the line, but it served its purpose at the time. After four decades of coexistence, with the British paying for a say over Afghan foreign policy, in 1919 under a new Amir, the Afghans invaded the North West Frontier province, threatening Peshawar. They were defeated in six months, in part by the use of a new weapon – air power.

The Great Game, meanwhile, had given birth to the first and, arguably, the most appealing of all great spy novels. In 1900, Rudyard Kipling started the publication of his novel *Kim*. The arch imperialist Kipling knew what he was talking about when it came to the grim realities of life on the North West Frontier, but he had also, from his childhood learning Hindi in Bombay and life as a journalist in the Punjab, developed a deep affection for and interest in the infinitely variegated people of India.

Appearing first in serial form, the story is that of an apparently ordinary, resourceful Indian child beggar, living on his wits in the streets of Lahore, who in fact is the orphan of an Irish foot soldier. 'Burned black as any native', he is 'white of the very poorest'. On becoming the *chela* (follower) of an ancient Tibetan lama who is looking for a magical river that can wash away all sins, they follow a vagabond life along the Grand Trunk Road, an extraordinary river of humanity, stretching all the way from Benares to Peshawar. A Pashtun horse-trader gives him a secret message to pass to the British head of the Indian Secret Service. As, on the road, he bumps into his father's regiment, he is identified and sent to an English school, resuming street life whenever he can and already acting as a junior participant in the Great Game, enabling him, while travelling again with the lama in the Himalayas, to steal valuable maps and papers from a Russian spy.

The importance and charm of *Kim* lies not in its rudimentary plot but in the characterisations of Kim and the lama and the relationship between them and its detailed, sensitive portrayal of the people, culture, religions and superstitions of India and of life in its streets and bazaars. Without being able to express his feelings, Kim finds it 'beautiful to watch the people, little clumps of red and blue and pink and white and saffron'. In the infinitely resourceful young 'imp' who, while considering him 'half mad', venerated his lama, Kipling had created an iconic figure. Nirad Chaudhuri considered it to be the best story in English about India. Set between the Second and Third Afghan Wars, it was the magnum opus of the Great Game, creating a legacy more powerful than that of any other spy novel and furnishing Philby with his familiar name.

* * *

Although born in Lancashire, Reginald Teague-Jones was brought up in St Petersburg, then at a German run school, becoming a competent linguist. In 1910, at the age of twenty-one, he joined the Indian Police and soon was transferred to the Indian government's Foreign and Political Department, which had trained some earlier figures in the Great Game. He became involved in intelligence gathering on the North West Frontier with Afghanistan, undertaking missions there and learning some Persian.

In 1917, he moved to the military intelligence headquarters in Delhi, where he was given responsibility for the Persian Gulf. With Russia disrupted by the revolution, the Turkish Army under Enver Pasha was making a rapid advance towards Baku. Teague-Jones was despatched to the area to assess the dangers to British interests. He crossed the Kopet Dag range in disguise to reach the small British garrison under General Malleson at Meshed in Turkestan. He spent the next six months between Meshed, Baku and Ashkhabad, where he found that the Bolsheviks had been overthrown by the Socialist Revolutionaries. He was appointed the British political representative in Ashgabat, as a small British force under Malleson arrived from Persia to support resistance to the Turks and fend off attacks by the Bolsheviks from Tashkent until the force withdrew early in 1919.

Teague-Jones's name was associated with the shooting of the twenty-six Bolshevik Commissars in Baku by their anti-Bolshevik Russian captors in September 1918. In 1919 and again in 1922, the Socialist Revolutionary lawyer, Vadim Chaikin, claimed that they had been killed on the orders of Teague-Jones, who wrote a lengthy rebuttal, which was passed by the British Foreign Office to the Soviet Commissariat for Foreign Affairs. Chaikin's account was endorsed by Trotsky and the Soviet regime, which did not save him later from being executed by the Bolsheviks. The massacre became the subject of a famous painting by Isaak Brodsky and then of a Soviet film.

In 1922, Teague-Jones, therefore, felt it prudent to adopt a new identity for the remaining sixty-six years of his life. He changed his name to Ronald Sinclair and all trace of him disappeared from the Foreign Office records. In 1926, he revisited Persia and published a record of the trip under his new name. He worked for MI5 as a Vice-Consul in New York from 1941 to the end of the war. It was only when he died in 1988, that Peter Hopkirk revealed his true identity as *The Spy Who Disappeared*, which, with Ronald Sinclair's *Diary of a Secret Mission to Russian Central Asia*, was published by Gollancz in 1990.

Colonel Frederick Bailey was a British intelligence officer, explorer in Tibet, zoologist, expert on high mountain butterflies and the Himalayan blue poppy. He joined Francis Younghusband in his brutal, unnecessary and unauthorised 1904 invasion of Tibet. But in 1910, he helped to rescue the Dalai Lama from the Chinese. His extraordinary account of his *Mission to Tashkent 1918*, published in 1946, is one of the greatest spy adventure books, far less well known than it deserves to be. He was despatched to Tashkent, on his own, to discover the intentions of the Bolsheviks, who were seizing power from the local khans. He also was supposed to monitor the activities of the Indian nationalist Mahendra Pratap, based in Kabul, who had been trying to persuade first the Germans and then the Bolsheviks to support an insurrection in India.

He survived for weeks in the Central Asian mountains on what he could shoot and cook for himself (with remarks about the excellence of the shooting). When, eventually, he was forced to descend into Baku, he found that the Bolsheviks had taken over and the ladies of his harem were enjoying being liberated from the Amir. Claiming to be an Azeri, to explain his heavily accented Russian, he contrived to get himself hired by the Bolshevik secret police, the *Cheka*. The assignment they gave him was to track down the Englishman in the area who was plotting against the Revolution! Despite being encumbered by a lady who insisted on taking her collection of valuable rugs with her, Bailey escaped across the Persian border, receiving a hero's welcome on his return to Britain.

The spirit of these adventurers was expressed by Robert Baden-Powell, who, disguised as a butterfly collector, worked for British military intelligence in the Mediterranean and received a medal for his scouting missions in Zululand. Similar exploits followed in Rhodesia and the Ashanti wars. Thereafter, apart from defending Mafeking, in disguise he undertook some of his own spying missions in the Anglo-Boer war. Ignoring the increasingly deadly nature of the 'game' they were all engaged in, this led him to declare, 'For anyone who is tired of life, the thrilling life of a spy would be the very finest recuperator.'

CHAPTER V

ERSKINE CHILDERS

Espionage, which, India apart, had been largely out of favour in Britain for the past two centuries, well and truly captured the public imagination again at the turn of the nineteenth and twentieth centuries as Kaiser Wilhelm II, though a grandchild of Queen Victoria, embarked on a flamboyant campaign of massive new German naval armaments and imperial ambitions, appearing ever more threatening to British interests.

Erskine Childers, born in 1870, was brought up in Ireland with his mother's family, who were Protestants at the time, but the family story was that his mother secretly had him christened as a Catholic. Having graduated in law from Cambridge, he became a clerk in Parliament. His great passion was sailing, graduating from a 'scrubby little yacht' to larger boats that he sailed first around England and Ireland and then to the Baltic and the Frisian islands off the coast of Germany, the Netherlands and Denmark. In 1899, he volunteered to serve in the Boer War in an artillery unit.

In 1897, the indefatigably inventive spy thriller writer William Le

Queux had published his first invasion scare book about supposed Franco-Russian plans to attack Britain. His fervent imagination and sometimes graphic turns of phrase ('That night, I slept but little') were later to earn him frequent references in Hugh and Graham Greene's entertaining *The Spy's Bedside Book*.

On his return to Britain in 1903, Erskine Childers went a long way better by publishing his hugely successful spy novel *The Riddle of the Sands: A Record of Secret Service*, which gave birth to a raft of others. The story is that of the narrator, Davies, and his friend in the Foreign Office, Carruthers, who is recovering from a failed love affair. Full of verifiable practical detail, setting a template for future spy novels, it describes how the narrator had become suspicious when he was nearly wrecked by a German boat luring him into a shoal in rough weather. He suspects the yacht's owner, Dollman, of being a renegade Englishman, but he has fallen in love with Dollman's daughter.

Having failed to interest the British authorities in the incident, Davies decides to investigate himself. When they approach a rumoured treasure recovery project on the island of Mehmet, they are warned away by a German patrol boat. They discover that Dollman had been a disgraced officer in the Royal Navy. It is only through superb seamanship in navigating the shoals, in a way the Germans do not believe possible, that they discover that the Germans are dredging channels through the shoals for barges to take an invasion force to Britain.

An 'epilogue' by the editor examines Dollman's plans for the invasion. A postscript states that the Royal Navy is finally taking countermeasures to intercept any German invasion force and urges haste. Childers declared that the book had been written 'for a purpose' and 'from a patriotic sense of duty'. On becoming First Lord of the Admiralty, Winston Churchill insisted on meeting the author. Churchill gave him credit for having awakened Britain to the seriousness of the threat from Germany.

In 1906, Lord Northcliffe's *Daily Mail* serialised *The Invasion of 1910* by Le Queux, forecasting a German invasion fleet sailing from the Frisian Islands. To whip up spy fever, actors were dressed up in German uniforms to walk down Piccadilly, with Le Queux estimating there to be fifty thousand German spies in Britain. When the active German spies were rounded up on the outbreak of the war, the number turned out to be twenty-two.

* * *

In 1904, Childers married a republican minded American, Mary Osgood, in Boston. She was credited with having contributed to his conversion from imperialism to Irish nationalism, but he was heading fast in that direction anyway. At the time, he was writing articles critical of British policy in South Africa and Ireland.

In 1908, the abject poverty he encountered on a journey through Western and Southwestern Ireland left him declaring on his return that he had 'finally and irrevocably' become a convert to full Home Rule for Ireland, despite having grown up 'steeped in' unreconcilable unionism. Though the Liberal Party supported Home Rule, he resigned from it in protest at the concessions being made to the Protestant Ulster Unionists.

In July 1914, in response to reports of the Ulster Unionists importing rifles and ammunition in Northern Ireland, Childers took the drastic step of using his yacht to smuggle guns bought in

Germany into Ireland in support of the nationalist Irish Volunteers (and some of the weapons supplied later were used by them in the 1916 Easter Rising). Yet in August that year he was admitted to the Royal Navy Volunteer Reserve. His first task was to work on whether it might be feasible for Britain to invade Germany – via the Frisian Islands! The potential for this, however, was rated by his superiors as nil, and the strategic significance of the islands in such shallow water also was rated as zero.

He became an instructor for new pilots in coastal navigation. His involvement in a bombing attack on the German airship base at Cuxhaven earned him a mention in despatches. He then served in a similar role in the Gallipoli campaign and the Eastern Mediterranean, earning a Distinguished Service Cross, returning to London in 1916 to receive his decoration from the King.

Meanwhile, on 21 April 1916, three days before the Easter Rising was due to take place, Sir Roger Casement was deposited on the Irish coast by a German submarine. Casement, who was born in Dublin, had served in the British consular service for more than twenty years. In the Congo, he met Joseph Conrad, who was writing *Heart of Darkness*. According to Casement, both believed that colonisation would bring progress to the continent and 'free its inhabitants from slavery, paganism and other barbarities'. According to Casement, 'Each would soon learn the gravity of his error.' Appointed by the British to investigate, he produced the Casement report on the horrendous human rights abuses in the Congo under the rule of the Belgian King Leopold. Subsequently, he wrote a similar report about the abuse of Peruvian Indians working on rubber plantations in the Amazon. In 1911, he was awarded a knighthood for his work on human rights.

In Ireland, in 1905, he became a sympathiser of the new Sinn Féin Party, which was campaigning for independence for a united Ireland, and a member of the paramilitary Irish Volunteers. In 1913, he resigned from the British consular service and travelled to the US to raise money for the Irish Volunteers, who he wanted to see arm themselves as some of the Unionists were doing.

In August 1914, on the outbreak of the First World War, he met the senior German diplomat Count Bernstorff in New York to propose that if Germany would sell guns to the Irish revolutionaries, the Irish would revolt, diverting troops away from the war with Germany. In October 1914, Casement sailed for Germany via Norway with a companion, Adler Christensen. In a meeting at the British legation in Norway, Christensen allegedly was offered a reward if Casement were 'knocked on the head.' A handwritten letter from a British diplomat, Mansfeldt Findlay, on paper from the British legation in Oslo, offered Christensen £5,000 plus immunity from prosecution and free passage to the United States in return for information leading to Casement's capture.

In November 1914, Casement negotiated a statement that Germany would never invade Ireland for conquest and was inspired by goodwill towards its people. He attempted to create an Irish brigade from the Irish prisoners captured by Germany in the early stages of the war, but only fifty-two of them were recruited. In April 1916, the Germans offered the Irish twenty thousand rifles and ten machine guns, with ammunition, but no direct military support, which was far short of what Casement was hoping for.

The German weapons never landed in England. The British having intercepted German communications, the Royal Navy boarded the ostensibly Norwegian but really German cargo vessel carrying them off Queenstown. The Irish trade unionists sent to unload them drove off a pier and drowned. The German captain scuttled his ship and the crew were taken prisoner.

By now convinced that the Germans would not provide adequate support for the rising, Casement tried to send a message to Dublin to urge postponement of the Easter rebellion, but the messenger he chose instead joined the Royal Navy. Put ashore in a pitiful condition with no support and suffering from malaria, Casement was immediately arrested and charged with treason, sabotage and espionage. Captured with him were his 'Black Diaries', revealing his homosexuality. The prosecutor, F. E. Smith, suggested to the defence that these could be used to enter a plea of insanity, but Casement refused to agree to this.

The Treason Act appeared only to apply to treasonous acts in Britain, not Germany, but the court decided that a comma should be read into the unpunctuated original Norman text, so that 'in the realm and elsewhere' referred to where actions took place and not just to where the King's enemies might be. The clarification led Casement to claim that he was being 'hanged for a comma!' Those who appealed for clemency included Sir Arthur Conan Doyle, W. B. Yeats, George Bernard Shaw and the US Senate but not Joseph Conrad, who could not forgive Casement his alliance with the Germans. Extracts from his diaries about his homosexuality were leaked to the press. When supporters appealed to the Free State Justice Minister, Kevin O'Higgins, he was dismissive of 'Englishmen who come to Ireland looking for excitement; we will make sure that they get some'. The appeal was rejected and Casement was hanged at Pentonville prison in August 1916.

The Easter Rising by twelve hundred Irish Volunteers, forcibly occupying many buildings in the centre of the city, including the General Post Office and City Hall, went ahead in Dublin from 24 to 29 April 1916, with the rebels hoisting flags and declaring an Irish Republic. The garrison initially were taken by surprise and pitched battles had to be fought to recover control of the key buildings. Nearly five hundred people were killed: 143 British military and police, eighty-two Irish rebels (including sixteen who were executed) and 260 civilians.

In 1965, the remains of Roger Casement were repatriated for a state funeral in Dublin. A flood of books and articles thereafter appeared about him, including a poem by Yeats about 'the ghost of Roger Casement beating on the door'.

In July 1917, Erskine Childers served as a secretary to a fruitless convention under Lloyd George about Irish Home Rule. He then was transferred back to the newly created Royal Air Force. He served as an intelligence officer studying first the navigational problems that would have been involved in an air attack on Berlin, then the effects of bombing in Belgium.

After the war, Childers met the Irish nationalist leaders Michael Collins and Éamon de Valera, president of Sinn Féin. The following year, he was elected to the Irish Parliament on behalf of Sinn Féin. He was secretary to the Irish delegation that negotiated the Anglo-Irish Treaty of 1921, creating an Irish Free State entirely independent of Britain but without the six counties dominated by the Protestant Ulster Unionists. As secretary to the delegation, his objections to independence without the six counties were overruled. At the conclusion of the negotiation, Lloyd George noted a 'sullen' Childers, disappointed that his 'sinister' attempts to wreck the negotiation had failed.

When Childers denounced the agreement in the Irish Parliament, Arthur Griffiths, one of the Sinn Féin leaders, alleged that he was secretly an English agent seeking to undermine the agreement and destabilise the new state. In reality, Irish nationalist leaders like Michael Collins had concluded, correctly, that Britain would not use force to oblige the Unionists to join an independent Ireland and the only way to achieve independence was to do so without the six counties.

This precipitated a civil war between the new Free State government and the Irish Republican Army (IRA). On 28 June 1922, using borrowed British artillery, the Free State forces bombarded the Four Courts in Dublin, which had been occupied as their military headquarters by the IRA. With the anti-Treaty forces in retreat, Childers became a fugitive, while still producing the IRA news sheet. The Free State's Justice Minister denounced Childers as the chief instigator of the rebellion. In September, Michael Collins was killed in an IRA ambush, leading to a declaration of martial law. Childers was arrested as he attempted to rejoin de Valera in Dublin. He was tried by a military court, accused of carrying a semi-automatic pistol. He was convicted and executed by firing squad. Before his execution, he shook hands with the firing squad and told them to take a step forward, saying, 'It will be easier that way.'

Winston Churchill declared that 'no man has done more harm or shown more genuine malice or endeavoured to bring a greater curse upon the common people of Ireland than this strange being, actuated by a deadly and malignant hatred for the land of his birth'. De Valera declared that 'he died the prince he was'.

His son, Erskine Hamilton Childers, became President of Ireland from 1973 until his death in office in the following year. Less written about than he merited, in 1974, Childers, the Irish revolutionary, was the subject of a biography by Andrew Boyle. His legacy was the template he had established for the modern spy novel, blending factual detail, imagination and plausibility, leaving his successors from John Buchan to le Carré following in his wake.

CHAPTER VI

WRITERS AND SPIES IN
THE FIRST WORLD WAR

Born in Scotland in 1875 and educated at Oxford, John Buchan was recruited as a member of the 'kindergarten' of bright young graduates assisting Lord Alfred Milner as the British High Commissioner in South Africa. As Private Secretary to Milner in the last year of the Second Anglo-Boer war, he saw all the main intelligence reports about Boer dispositions and intentions. Thereafter, the focus was on reconciliation and economic revival of the Free State and the Transvaal.

On return to Britain, although trained as a barrister, his passion was writing. His first book was a successful African adventure story, *Prester John*, about a rebellion inspired by the legend of a mythical leader. Then, a few months into the First World War, he published what has remained one of the world's best loved spy adventure novels, *The Thirty-Nine Steps*, about a German attempt to discover Britain's naval secrets. The plot lacked the apparent plausibility of

The Riddle of the Sands but featured a thoroughly British, stiff upper lip, immensely resourceful hero called Richard Hannay.

Alerted to a German plot by a stranger who then is murdered in his apartment, Hannay is pursued to Scotland by the police and the Germans, with a spectacular scene of him being chased across the Scottish moors by a primitive bi-plane. On return, he finds that a Foreign Office dignitary has divulged British naval secrets to a bilingual German. Deciphering his informant's code book, he finds that it refers to thirty-nine steps, which he works out must refer to the number of steps to the sea from their getaway villa. The villa is identified and the Germans arrested in the nick of time.

The book and its hero, with its 'man on the run' theme, got a huge following in wartime Britain, including among the men in the trenches, and thereafter withstood the test of time, as Buchan had invented a precursor to James Bond in his also iconically British, though far more *pukka*, old style hero. The result was a series of films, the best and most popular of which, directed by Alfred Hitchcock in 1935, featured Robert Donat, with Madeleine Carroll supplying a love interest that was absent from the novel. Further successful film versions followed with Kenneth More in 1959 and John Mills in 1978 and then by the BBC in 2008.

Buchan's next spy novel, *Greenmantle*, published in 1916, is the dramatic story, full of twists, turns and exotic locations, of the attempts the Germans really were making to raise an Islamic rebellion against Britain in the Middle East and India. Hannay and his Boer friend, Pieter Pienaar, recruited as pretend sympathisers of the Germans, meet their leader, Ulrich von Stumm. Then, with Sandy Arbuthnot, he meets the co-leader, Hilda von Einem, who develops a soft spot for them.

Sandy discovers that the prophet named Greenmantle is dying and decides to impersonate him. Cornered by the Turks, Hannay is rescued by whirling dervishes, whose leader turns out to be Sandy! They capture the German plans and cross the battlefield to give them to the Russians just in time to help them win the battle of Erzurum.

With the Russians featuring as allies, the book was read by the imperial royal family amidst the Russian revolution. The first chapter of the book, *A Mission is Proposed*, was included by Graham Greene in his 1957 anthology *The Spy's Bedside Book*.

Buchan, meanwhile, was serving in military intelligence with the British Army in France but then was appointed director of information for the remainder of the war, becoming later Governor General of Canada and, by then, the author of fifty books. Some of the early critics of Ian Fleming's works deplored the fact that his creation, James Bond, was so much less of a proper English gentleman than Richard Hannay.

* * *

While John Buchan was writing books, Compton Mackenzie was functioning as a real wartime spy for Britain in Greece. He was commissioned in the Royal Marines, but as he suffered from poor health, he was assigned to counter-intelligence work during the Gallipoli campaign. In 1916, with Greece neutral at the time, he built up a counter-intelligence network in Athens.

Although a favourite of 'C', Sir Mansfield Smith-Cumming, he was not under effective control by anyone. He was alleged to have been involved in an attempt to assassinate the pro-German King of Greece, Constantine I, by poisoning him. He was a supporter and funder of the Liberal Party leader Eleftherios Venizelos, who supported the allies. His support for the Venizelists led him to be expelled from Greece in 1916. But in the following year, he founded the Aegean Intelligence Service and ran it pretty much as he pleased. He was recalled from Greece in September 1917. The Venizelists having gained the upper hand, Constantine was forced to abdicate and Greece joined the allies.

Smith-Cumming wanted to appoint Mackenzie as his deputy but faced a revolt by his staff over this. Mackenzie was awarded the OBE plus the *Légion d'Honneur* and a similar Greek honour. On the publication of his *Greek Memories* in 1932, he was prosecuted under the Official Secrets Act for supposedly quoting from secret documents. He was given a fine of £100 plus prosecution costs, but his own costs were over £1,000 – a significant sum at the time. He asked which passages the authorities objected to and a new version was published without them. The unexpurgated version had already been deposited at the British Museum, but it was made impossible for anyone to access it! It was eventually republished, including the censored passages, in 2012 by Biteback.

* * *

There were some subsequent attempts to question the contribution T. E. Lawrence made to the 1916–18 Arab Revolt against Germany's allies, the Turks, but that was emphatically not the view of General Allenby, Britain's successful commander in the Middle East. He approved Lawrence's strategy of using the Bedouin forces as irregulars, with hit and run tactics and not trying to form them into normal army units. 'I gave him a free hand ... I never had anything but praise for his work, which indeed was invaluable throughout the campaign. He was the mainspring of the Arab movement and knew their language, their manners and their mentality.'

T. E. Lawrence was born in 1888, out of wedlock, to Sir Thomas Chapman and Sarah Junner, a governess. His parents thereafter lived together, adopting the surname of Lawrence. Lawrence graduated from Oxford, and from 1910 to 1914, he worked for the British Museum as an archaeologist, mainly in Syria, where he learned some Arabic and already was in contact with British intelligence. On the outbreak of war, he joined the British Arab Bureau's intelligence unit in Cairo.

Headed by Sharif Hussein, the Emir of Mecca, there was a growing Arab nationalist movement within the Ottoman territories and Lawrence was sympathetic to it. In 1916, he was sent to Mesopotamia in an unsuccessful attempt to relieve the siege of Kut by encouraging an Arab uprising. Meanwhile, without the knowledge of the British officials in Cairo, Britain and France were negotiating the Sykes/Picot agreement confirming French claims to much of Syria, though accepting that there could also be some independent Arab territory there if the Arabs themselves liberated it.

The Arab Revolt began in 1916 but got bogged down, with a risk that the Turks might recapture Mecca. Lawrence, sent to interview Sharif Hussain's three sons, concluded that Faisal was best equipped to lead the revolt. Faisal and Lawrence developed a plan to threaten the railway from Syria and, rather than trying to take the second holy city of Medina, to block the Turkish forces there.

Lawrence was due to be replaced, but Faisal asked that his position should be made permanent. While acting as Faisal's principal adviser on strategy, he participated personally in a series of attacks on the railway, bridges and Ottoman outposts. In 1917, he made a three hundred mile journey to meet Arab nationalists near Damascus, advising them to await the arrival of Faisal's forces.

In November that year, he was captured briefly by the Turks and subjected to torture and, he implied, rape. In helping to plan the successful capture of the port of Aqaba, he did not tell his superiors in case the French tried to block it. The rout of Ottoman forces in the January 1918 battle of Talifah was considered a 'brilliant feat of arms', for which Lawrence was awarded the Distinguished Service Order. By this time, he had been promoted to full colonel.

Their differences over Syria had caused him to be denounced as anti-French. Nevertheless, he was awarded the *Légion d'Honneur* and the *Croix de Guerre*. He attended the Paris Peace Conference as a member of Faisal's delegation then worked for a year for his admirer Winston Churchill at the Colonial Office.

The American writer and film maker, Lowell Thomas, had shot dramatic footage of Lawrence in Arab robes during his time in the desert. After the war, he produced a stage representation of 'Lawrence in Arabia' that made Lawrence a household name.

To the astonishment of his friends, who included John Buchan, E. M. Forster, Joseph Conrad and Augustus John, in 1922, Lawrence enlisted in the RAF as an ordinary aircraftman under the pseudonym Ross, later changed to Shaw, apparently in reference to his friendship with George Bernard Shaw. His account of his life in the RAF was published after his death as *The Mint*.

In 1926, he produced a private edition of his memoir, *Seven Pillars of Wisdom*, a published version of which immediately became a bestseller. George Bernard Shaw helped him to edit it. Apart from the enthralling story, it was written in a very distinctive, florid style. It was republished many times, including after his death. But in his lifetime Lawrence refused to make any money from it, donating the proceeds to the RAF Benevolent Fund. He was killed in a motorcycle accident in 1935.

In a 'deleted chapter' of the *Seven Pillars*, written in 1924, he wrote, 'The Cabinet raised the Arabs to fight for us by definite promises of self-government afterwards.' He had endorsed their promises. They had performed some fine things together, but he now felt bitterly ashamed of the broken promises.

In 1955, Richard Aldington, who considered the Arabs not to be ready for full self-government, did an attempted demolition job on the *Seven Pillars*, which he described as a work of quasi-fiction, and on Lawrence' s character, revealing his illegitimacy and implying homosexuality. In reality, no evidence exists that Lawrence ever had consensual sex with anyone, male or female. The *Seven Pillars* contained a long, graphic description of his torture by the Turks and it did indeed contain some exaggerations of the role he had played, plus some figments of his imagination, but Aldington's attack triggered an indignant rebuttal from other commentators, led by the military historian Basil Liddell Hart, affirming the vital role Lawrence had played in the Arab revolt.

The Lawrence of Arabia legend had long since been solidly established. The 1962 David Lean film, featuring exceptional photography and a virtuoso performance by Peter O'Toole, came high in the rankings as one of the best films ever made, which was what the story of, arguably, the most extraordinary of all British secret agents deserved.

CHAPTER VII

THE 'ACE OF SPIES' AND RUSSIA

R obert Bruce Lockhart was born in Scotland in 1887 and educated at Fettes College in Edinburgh. His mother was a McGregor, enabling him to claim that there was not a drop of English blood in his veins. At twenty-one he went to Malaya to work on rubber plantations owned by his uncles. He caused a 'minor sensation' by carrying off Amai, the beautiful ward of a local Malay prince. He returned to Britain to pass the Foreign Service examination and was posted to Moscow in 1912.

He was the acting Consul General in Moscow throughout most of the First World War from 1914 to 1917, arriving back in London six weeks before the Bolshevik Revolution. He was turned around and sent back to Moscow as the UK's first envoy to the Bolsheviks, not as an ambassador but as the 'head of a special mission'. Lockhart also was working for the Secret Intelligence Service, who gave him £648 worth of diamonds to fund an agent network. In his subsequent bestseller, *Memoirs of a British Agent*, he gave his account of the 1918 'Lockhart Plot' to overthrow the Bolshevik regime.

His principal associate in trying to do so, Sidney Reilly, the supposed 'ace of spies', was born Zigmund Rozenblum in Odessa in 1874. He was employed by Scotland Yard's Special Branch and the British Secret Service Bureau, precursor of MI6, and later also by the British War Office. He was alleged to have spied for at least four different countries and was fluent in several languages. He was involved in spying on Russian émigrés in London in the 1890s for the Tsarist secret service, the *Okhrana*.

Much of Reilly's career is obscure, but his record was that of an adventurer and possibly a criminal. In 1898, he had an affair with a British woman, whose husband then died in suspicious circumstances, leaving her £800,000. When they got married, he changed his name to Sidney Reilly. He then became a spy for the Japanese on the eve of the Russo-Japanese war, while also working for the British. Amidst lax Russian security, he gave the Japanese valuable information about the defences of Port Arthur and was well rewarded by them.

On his return to Europe, he worked for William Melville, Superintendent of Scotland Yard's Special Branch and chief of a new intelligence section in the War Office. He helped Melville to persuade an Australian mining engineer, William D'Arcy, at the last minute, to sell an important oil concession in Persia to Britain, not France. He was sent to Germany to spy on the Krupp munitions plant in Essen. In 1912, he returned to St Petersburg, resuming contact with the *Okhrana*, probably as a double agent. He spent the first two years of the First World War in the United States, where he approached the British intelligence representatives in New York, who recommended him to Mansfield Smith-Cumming and for a commission in the Canadian Royal Flying Corps. The award to him later of a Military Cross (MC) led it to be supposed that he served with the British forces in the First World War, which was not the case.

In spring 1918, Smith-Cumming formally enlisted Reilly in MI6 and sent him to St Petersburg (by then Petrograd). He regarded him as 'a rascal' but planned to 'get what use I could out of him'. Reilly resumed contact with his *Okhrana* contact, Grammatikov, who said that the Russian government was now in the hands of the criminal classes and of 'lunatics released from the asylums'. He arranged a contact with a secretary of the Council of People's Commissars, with Reilly pretending to be a Bolshevik sympathiser, enabling him to get a permit from their spy organisation, the *Cheka*. When it came to the so called Ambassadors' Plot or Lockhart/ Reilly plot, Lockhart confessed that he did not himself know fully the role Reilly had played.

Reilly had established contacts with the remaining anti-Bolshevik forces linked to Kerensky's Deputy Minister of Defence and the Socialist Revolutionary Party, who the British supported with secret funds, also with some involvement by the French and American representatives in Moscow and Petrograd. Dissident elements of the Latvian regiment protecting Lenin were in touch with Reilly and the British naval attaché, Captain Francis Cromie. The plan was to try to seize Lenin and Trotsky at a meeting in early September, reasoning that, without them, the Bolsheviks would fall apart.

Lockhart stood back from the plot, delegating planning to Reilly, who he described as having great energy and personal charm.

Though he didn't find him exceptionally intelligent, he felt that 'his courage and indifference to danger were superb'. The commander of the Latvian contingent, however, had reported Reilly's approach to the head of the *Cheka*, Felix Dzerzhinsky.

There were persistent rumours of an Allied military intervention. On 4 August 1918, an allied force landed at Archangel, ostensibly to safeguard military supplies from the Germans. Reilly's plan was to stage a coup during the meeting of the Council of Peoples' Commissars in early September. He was able to travel to Petrograd using his *Cheka* credentials. On 30 August, the Socialist Revolutionary plotters ordered a military cadet to kill the head of the Petrograd *Cheka*. On the same day, another socialist revolutionary, Fanya Kaplan, shot and very nearly killed Lenin. The attacks were used by Dzerzhinsky to unleash the 'Red Terror', involving mass executions and an attack on the British Consulate in which Cromie was killed trying to protect it.

Accused of being the main instigator of the plot, Lockhart, on his arrest, was placed in the same cell as Fanya Kaplan. He had never had any contact with her and she showed no sign of recognition, but Lockhart for a time felt himself to be in imminent danger of execution. Instead, the British government managed to get him exchanged for the Bolshevik representative in London, Maxim Litvinov, who they had arrested for propaganda.

Most of those implicated in the coup attempt, including Reilly's two Russian mistresses, were arrested and tortured. Fanya Kaplan and several others were executed. Rilley's MI6 contact, who provided him with false papers, enabling him to escape, reported him as being calm and collected and keen to try again! Tried *in absentia*,

Lockhart and Reilly were sentenced to death, with the sentence to be carried out if they ever returned to Russia.

Within a week of their return to Britain, Reilly and his MI6 contact, Captain Hill, were sent back to Southern Russia as British trade representatives, the real purpose being to support the White Russian and other anti-Bolshevik forces there. The MC was awarded to him in 1919 for his work in this period behind Russian lines. Thereafter, Reilly may have been involved in the fabrication of the letter from the Comintern official, Zinoviev, the publication of which helped to scupper the Labour Party's chances of winning the 1924 British general election.

In that year, he was invited to Finland by a supposedly anti-Bolshevik organisation known as 'the Trust'. Once there, he was introduced to purportedly anti-Bolshevik figures who, in reality, were agents of Dzerzhinsky's OGPU. Escorted across the border by a Finnish OGPU agent, he was arrested, interrogated and shot in a forest near Moscow on 5 November 1925.

His 'ace of spies' legend thereafter gained huge publicity in the world press. Bruce Lockhart's *Memoirs of a British Agent* was made into a movie by Warner Brothers. Lockhart believed in several tales of Reilly's prior derring-do for which there was little evidence but corroborated his efforts to try to overthrow the Bolsheviks, which made Reilly famous, including in Russia, where several films were made about the regime's success in thwarting his attempted coup.

He has continued to be a source of fascination for authors attempting the near hopeless task of determining which parts of the legend were based on fact and how much he actually achieved. But he was admired by his British controllers as a vastly experienced, courageous and resourceful agent who always had a plan or was working on one but who could be reckless, as he was in the plot against Lenin and in allowing himself to be lured across the Finnish border. He underestimated his opponents who, by this time, had thoroughly infiltrated *émigré* circles.

*　*　*

Bruce Lockhart left the Foreign Service and intelligence work to concentrate on his writing. Meanwhile, Arthur Ransome, the future author of *Swallows and Amazons*, was attracting the attention of MI5. In 1913, Ransome went to Russia to study its folklore. From the following year, he became a foreign correspondent for the radical *Daily News*. Bruce Lockhart described him as a 'Don Quixote with a walrus moustache, a sentimentalist who could always be relied upon to champion the underdog and a visionary whose imagination had been fired by the revolution'. He was on excellent terms with Lenin and Trotsky and, with an unhappy marriage in England, was having an affair with Trotsky's statuesque secretary, Evgenia Shelepina. His articles, especially those opposing Allied intervention, were regarded by MI5 as 'near treasonous'. In 1919, he was summoned to a meeting in England with Reginald Leeper of the Foreign Office's Political Intelligence Department who, to Ransome's indignation, demanded that he should submit his articles in advance for approval.

In 1919, when he returned to Moscow on behalf of *The Guardian*, the Estonian Foreign Minister entrusted him to deliver a secret armistice proposal to the Bolsheviks. To preserve secrecy, this was not written down, with the Estonians relying on Ransome's reputation to get it taken seriously. Having crossed the battle lines on foot,

Ransome passed the message to Maxim Litvinov in Moscow. To deliver the positive reply, Ransome had to return by the same risky means, this time with Evgenia alongside him.

Bruce Lockhart saved Ransome from further attention from MI5 by revealing to them that Ransome was providing information to the Secret Intelligence Service with the code name S.76. MI5's suspicions were not entirely unfounded as, later, Evgenia sold in Paris some diamonds from the Bolsheviks to help their financing. After his divorce, Arthur Ransome married Evgenia and they spent some years sailing in the Baltic. On their return to England, the bestselling *Swallows and Amazons* series of books began to be published in 1930.

*   *   *

By 1914, Somerset Maugham was an extremely successful playwright with, at one point, four of his plays running in London at the same time. He was regarded by patronising British critics as merely an entertainer, though he was by then on the verge of publishing his masterpiece, *Of Human Bondage*. Too old for military service, he volunteered to serve in France as an ambulance driver for the British Red Cross. Having been educated at Berlin University, he was fluent also in French. He was recruited by Sir John Wallinger, formerly head of security in India, to the Secret Intelligence Service, for whom he worked whenever required throughout the war. As a patriotic gesture, he insisted on doing so at his own expense. He first moved to Geneva, from where, presenting himself as a French playwright and in defiance of Swiss neutrality laws, he relayed to London reports from British agents in enemy territory.

In November 1916, he was despatched to the Pacific to report on German activities in the region, including the powerful radio transmitter they had built in Samoa. In August 1917, he was sent by Sir William Wiseman of SIS to Petrograd to try to encourage the moderate Kerensky regime and to counter German propaganda as Russia came closer to withdrawing from the war. He was supposed to do so in the guise of a journalist working for an American magazine.

As Maugham wrote later, 'I was sent to prevent the Bolshevik Revolution and keep Russia in the war. The reader will know that my efforts did not meet with success.'

Helped by his former mistress, Sasha Kropotkin, he had a series of meetings with Kerensky, entertaining him or his ministers regularly over vodka and caviar at the most expensive restaurant in Petrograd. Unsurprisingly at the time, he found that the Russians 'take their liquor sadly. They weep when they are drunk. They are very often drunk.' He was unimpressed by Kerensky, who was pessimistic about his prospects and seemed to him to lack both magnetism and vigour.

Their meetings ended dramatically when, on 31 October 1917, Kerensky gave him a letter to deliver to Lloyd George with a desperate request to the Allies to raise an anti-Bolshevik army. When Maugham gave this to Lloyd George, he was dismissed with, 'I am afraid I cannot do that; and I have a Cabinet meeting to attend.' It was far too late anyway. By November, Kerensky had been overthrown and the Bolsheviks were in control.

The war over, Maugham wrote a number of stories about his secret experiences, submitting them all for clearance, as he was legally bound to do. As a result, several were suppressed, but the remainder were published in his 1928 book *Ashenden*, making him the first British intelligence agent to publish a book about his experiences as one – four years ahead of Compton Mackenzie. One of the characters in it is named Somerville, after Maugham's alias in Russia. Wallinger features in it as 'R.' It contains various invented episodes, but also an account of his adventures in Russia. Oleg Gordievsky proved to be an admirer of *Ashenden*, commending it to a fellow KGB officer, on the eve of his escape from Russia.

Maugham much preferred the role of a writer to that of a spy. In the foreword to *Ashenden*, he wrote that 'The role of a spy in the Intelligence Department is on the whole monotonous. A lot of it is uncommonly useless.' Undoubtedly, he was right about that, but his assignment in Russia had not been monotonous at all.

Scarred by the fate of Oscar Wilde, Maugham feared a similar fate if he remained in Britain. So he resumed his travels, especially in the Pacific, before moving with his long term male companion to Cap Ferrat. *Of Human Bondage* was followed by *The Moon and Sixpence*, *Cakes and Ale* and other bestsellers, while his short stories about the Far East also helped to make him one of the most successful British authors ever. Critics remained irritated by the absence of any deeper pretensions, but none could ever question his extraordinary readability. Reportedly the best-paid writer of the 1930s, he has remained the one with the most (nearly a hundred) British film and TV adaptations of his work.

CHAPTER VIII

MI5 AND MI6

It was not until the approach of the First World War that the rudimentary British intelligence services were reorganised into a system seeking to become comparable in its effectiveness to that of Francis Walsingham.

From 1795, the Royal Navy Hydrographic Department had started developing charts that eventually enveloped the world, displaying the positions of all British ships with, later, those of many foreign ships too. The introduction of the telegraph cable by Samuel Morse transformed the ability to communicate with, from the 1870s, the establishment of a worldwide system of transatlantic and other cables under British control.

In 1887, Commander Henry Hall became the first director of naval intelligence. His son was to become the greatest ever holder of the post. From 1909, Colonel (later Sir) Vernon Kell was appointed director of a new Secret Service Bureau created in response to fears that the Germans living in Britain were or would become spies. Mansfield Smith-Cumming was a naval officer assigned to shore duties with naval intelligence because he suffered from seasickness. Vernon Kell supervised the home section and Smith-Cumming the foreign section of the new Secret Service Bureau, which then became known, respectively, as MI5 and the Secret Intelligence Service (SIS), or MI6. By 1914, the Foreign Intelligence Committee had been formed, bringing together representatives of the Navy, Army and Foreign Office, precursor of the current Joint Intelligence Committee.

Over the next few years, Smith-Cumming became known as 'C' because of his habit of signing documents with a C, later written in green ink. The habit has persisted in MI6, though the 'C' now stands for 'chief'. The practice was borrowed by Ian Fleming, though designating the Chief as 'M', rather than 'C'.

In 1914, Smith-Cumming was involved in a serious road accident in France, in which his son was killed. He claimed later to have cut off his leg with a penknife to escape from the car. In fact, his foot was amputated in hospital. Invariably wearing a gold monocle, he would interrupt meetings in his office by suddenly stabbing himself in the foot with a knife or letter opener. He also was reputed to use a wooden scooter, with his good leg serving to propel himself faster along the office corridors. He had an 'infectious enthusiasm' for gadgets, invisible inks and the paraphernalia of spying, which he regarded as 'capital sport'.

The most immediate achievement of British intelligence in the First World War was the very rapid neutralisation by MI5 and the Special Branch of the police under Sir Basil Thomson of the German spy network in the United Kingdom, with twenty-two immediate arrests, eleven of whom were executed. Overseas networks were given less priority and were far less developed than in the

Second World War, apart from the Belgian *'Dame Blanche'* intelligence network. The dogged battles in the trenches did not favour intelligence work. But it was precisely at this point that a new brand of intelligence started to display the supremacy it has enjoyed ever since.

The first director's son, Admiral Sir Reginald 'Blinker' Hall, was the British director of naval intelligence from 1914 to 1919. Together with Sir Alfred Ewing, he established the Royal Navy's code breaking operation, based in Room 40 of the Admiralty. He had previously used a cadet training ship to photograph facilities in German ports. Before the war, two of his officers were captured and imprisoned for a time for espionage in Germany. As later was the case at Bletchley Park, he assembled a code breaking team that brought together people from very different walks of life – university professors, stockbrokers and bankers, and even a clergyman.

The first demonstration of the power of this relatively new brand of intelligence came in relation to Ireland. It was thanks to their intercepts that the Germans were unable to land arms and Sir Roger Casement was captured in Tralee Bay in April 1916. Hall was aware of the imminent Easter Rising but refused to reveal his sources, so his warning was not taken sufficiently seriously. The intercepts also led to the arrest of the key German field agent in the US, Captain Franz von Rintelen, who had financed and encouraged labour strikes, sabotaged munitions factories and tried to take over the DuPont Corporation.

In January 1917, the Zimmermann telegram was despatched by Arthur Zimmermann of the German Foreign Office, instructing their ambassador there to inform the Mexicans that if they entered the war against the United States, with Germany's aid they could expect to recover Texas, Arizona and New Mexico. The telegram was sent in anticipation of the resumption by the Germans of unrestricted submarine warfare on 1 February, which they expected to lead to war with the United States.

Unbeknownst to the Germans, the telegram went via Stockholm to Buenos Aires, over British submarine cables, en route to Mexico. At the same time, it was transmitted via the US Ambassador in Germany, as President Wilson had allowed the Germans to use US diplomatic channels to send 'peace' messages.

In Room 40, Nigel de Grey had partly decoded the message by the next day. The German diplomatic code 13040 was familiar to Room 40, who also were able to decipher German naval traffic. But Hall was reluctant to release the transcript as that would reveal that Room 40 could read German cypher traffic (and the diplomatic traffic of the United States). Hall waited three weeks while de Grey and his colleague, William Montgomery, completed the decryption. On 5 February, he passed the telegram to the Foreign Office but still warned against using it. The British needed a cover story to enable them to do so, which was provided by an agent obtaining a copy of the encoded text from the Mexican telegraph office.

Hall showed the telegram to Edward Bell in the US Embassy on 19 February, then to the US Ambassador, Walter Page, on the 20th. On 23 February the Foreign Secretary, Arthur Balfour, gave Page the coded text, the message in German and the English translation, saying that it had been obtained in Mexico. The Americans were given the code 13040 code to verify it.

Page informed President Wilson on the 24th. The telegram was published on 1 March. On 3 March, Zimmermann confirmed that it was genuine. The Americans had agreed to use the Mexican telegraph office cover story. It was Page who described Admiral Hall as 'a clear case of genius'.

On 1 February, the Germans had resumed unrestricted submarine warfare against ships bearing the American flag and two were sunk in February. The telegram had referred to the intended 'ruthless employment of our submarines'. It was the attacks by German submarines that forced the US into the war, but the publication of the Zimmermann telegram certainly helped. It is difficult to think of a single piece of cryptanalysis that had a more dramatic effect. On 6 April 1917, Congress voted to declare war on Germany.

It was in this period that the youthful US Navy Secretary, Franklin Delano Roosevelt, reached the conclusion that 'the British intelligence unit [was] far ahead of ours'. 'Blinker' Hall even tried to convince him that one of his agents regularly visited the German naval base at Kiel (not actually true!). But his experiences at this time helped to convince him in the Second World War that a new US intelligence system needed to be created in association with the British.

'Blinker' Hall would rather have perished than publish a memoir and there was no question of anyone else at the time writing a book about Room 40. Although, of course, it was understood that efforts had been and were under way to decipher adversaries' codes, the secret of how much success had been achieved in actually doing so was far better kept after the First World War than proved possible after the second, when the extraordinary achievements of the Bletchley Park cryptographers ended up being publicised more than most of them would ever have wished.

*   *   *

Fitzroy Maclean was born into the Scottish clan of that name in 1911. A member of the Diplomatic Service, in 1937 he volunteered to be posted to Moscow, where he was present during the Stalinist purges of Bukharin and most of the other leading early Bolsheviks. As he recounted in the first part of his memoir *Eastern Approaches*, he managed to travel, mainly by train, to remote regions of the Soviet Union, which were supposed to be banned to foreigners, with the NKVD in hot pursuit.

In 1939, when war broke out, he found that, as a member of the Diplomatic Service, he could not join the army. So he resigned, supposedly to go into politics. Instead, he took a taxi to the nearest recruiting office and enlisted as a private in the Queen's Own Cameron Highlanders. In North Africa in 1942, he became a key member of the newly formed Special Air Service (SAS), developing ways of driving vehicles over the Libyan desert, behind Rommel's forces on the coast. Transferred to what is now Iran, he was instructed to kidnap General Zahedi, the commander of the pro-German Iranian forces in Isfahan. He did so, smuggling him out to internment by the British in Palestine.

In 1943, Churchill chose him to lead a mission to Yugoslavia. Josip Tito and his partisans were emerging as the main threat to the German occupying forces there. Little was known about Tito. Maclean's task was to get to know and support him, though he was a committed communist and the British, hitherto, had been supporting the much weaker Royalist forces there under General Mihailović.

Churchill told Maclean not to concern himself with how Yugoslavia was to be run after the war, but 'simply to find out who was killing the most Germans and suggest means by which we could help them to kill more'. In the summer of 1944, in concert with Tito, he planned a major bombing campaign to impede the German forces there being withdrawn to reinforce those fighting against the Allies in Central Europe. A great admirer of Tito, he subsequently wrote two books about him.

For his efforts in Yugoslavia, Maclean was promoted to Major General and received honours from Tito, the French and the Russians, as well as the British. He was encouraged by Tito to buy a house on the Dalmatian island of Korčula. Though a communist, to the fury of Stalin, Tito refused to accept Soviet oversight of Yugoslavia. The assistance he had received from the Western allies during the war had encouraged him to pursue his own, independent foreign policy. Maclean published numerous books about his adventures and travel, but it was his war exploits recorded in *Eastern Approaches* that earned him lasting fame.

CHAPTER IX

GRAHAM GREENE

Graham Greene, who worked for MI6 during the war, was obsessed with the world of espionage. No fewer than four of his books were spy novels and virtually all the others are characterised by episodes of deception and betrayal. He contended that both the writer and the spy needed the same quality – 'a splinter of ice in the heart'. Greene, notoriously, befriended his former MI6 mentor, Kim Philby, all over again *after* he had betrayed all his colleagues and country, contributing a foreword to Philby's memoir, *My Silent War*. He was notorious also for his torrid affair with his fellow Catholic goddaughter, the extremely beautiful Catherine Walston, immortalised by him in *The End of the Affair*.

Graham Greene had an unhappy childhood. His disciplinarian father was also headmaster at his boarding school, Berkhamsted, leaving him little space to breathe. He was bullied by two boys, Carter and Wormold (whose names he subsequently used in *Our Man in Havana*), leaving him depressed and attempting to commit suicide in the nearby woods with handfuls of aspirins and by eating deadly nightshade. He claimed also to have played Russian roulette there with a loaded pistol. His brother, however, who lived with him, reported that there was indeed a pistol, but with no bullets in it. At sixteen, he spent six months under psychoanalysis. He subsequently was diagnosed as manic depressive. Studying history at Balliol College, Oxford, he often seemed moody and depressed. 'He looked down on us', wrote Evelyn Waugh, 'and shared in none of our revelry.' In 1922, he was briefly a member of the British Communist Party.

While he was working as a sub-editor on the *Times*, his future wife, Vivien, wrote to him to correct an obscure point of Catholic doctrine. As he got close to marrying her, the then agnostic Greene thought that he had better get to know the beliefs she held, immersing himself in a crash course in Catholic theology. Father Trollope persuaded him to be baptised as a Catholic. But, so far as Greene was concerned, this was on the basis of the 'what if' there is a higher being? The believer then has a better chance of being saved, and if there isn't, it doesn't matter. Having led a life of often spectacular debauchery, Greene asked to see a priest just before he died. Having married Vivien, he subsequently told her that he was totally unsuited to family life.

In his memoir, *A Sort of Life*, Greene recounted his first, unserious student foray into espionage. For, in 1924, while still at Oxford, he volunteered to work for German nationalists in the Ruhr, then occupied by the French. Seeing them as the underdogs suffering from defeat, he wrote to the German Embassy proposing himself as a spy and propagandist on their behalf. His life then seemed for a while to be 'filled by Germans'. He left for the Ruhr with twenty-five pounds from the German Embassy and his friend, Claud Cockburn. Neither took the assignment the least bit seriously. They tried to find examples of Senegalese occupying troops behaving badly but failed to do so. They met a 'shady' German in plus fours who tried to kidnap his countrymen collaborating with the French to face trial in Germany. Greene started planning a thriller 'rather in the Buchan manner'. When he suggested to the Germans that he should go back to the Ruhr as a proper spy, he was thrilled that they accepted the offer. At that age, he wrote, 'I was ready to be a mercenary in any cause so long as I was repaid with excitement and a little risk.'

While working for *The Times*, to shrug off the plague of boredom and in search of new sensations, he travelled as extensively as he could, visiting in Mexico both a brothel and a monastery. His interests at the time were described as 'drink, opium, adventure and beautiful women'. There was, he said, no danger of him becoming a priest: 'Chastity would have been beyond my powers.'

Greene's sister worked for MI6. In 1941, she persuaded him to join them too. He was despatched to the unimportant backwater of Sierra Leone. He was trained in the tedious processes of the personal coding and decoding of messages and how to use invisible ink. He was given some very basic army training so that, when necessary, 'he would not look out of place in khaki.' His fellow agent, John le Carré, meeting him in Freetown, found him convulsed with laughter at the fact that the service still had references in its code books to eunuchs, presumably to gather information from harems!

Greene had little success trying to run agents in the neighbouring French speaking countries, under Vichy's control. He received a report that the Vichy French airport in Guinea supposedly had a large building that contained a tank. He told his superiors that he suspected it was just a warehouse and the author of the report was illiterate. So he was surprised that his report was rated 'most valuable'. It was, he said later, this episode in his 'little shack in Freetown, remembered in a Club in St. James's', that helped first to give him the idea for *Our Man in Havana*.

He returned to MI6 in London to work, under Kim Philby, on the Abwehr's efforts at subversion in Portugal. He found that some of the Abwehr agents in Portugal were 'sending home completely erroneous reports received from imaginary agents. It was a paying game.' One of the agents, called GARBO, a Spanish double agent in Lisbon, pretended to control a network of agents all over England. He invented military movements and operations from maps and guides. GARBO was an inspiration for Wormold in *Our Man in Havana*.

From 1946 to 1950, he had an incandescent affair with Catherine Walston. *The End of the Affair*, published in 1951, was dedicated to 'C'; the US edition was dedicated to 'Catherine'. Having got married very young, she had introduced herself to Greene by writing to him about her interest in converting to Catholicism and was adopted as his goddaughter. The novel features the London restaurant Rules, which was where their affair started, and 'onions', which was their code for making love. Harry Walston, though prepared to overlook his wife's infidelities, was furious and mortified to have one publicised in this manner. Greene would have wished to decamp with Catherine, but he proved to have met his match in her, as her lovers included an American general and a former IRA chieftain. Reputedly, she also enjoyed defrocking priests.

In April 1950, he wrote to tell her that he had confessed all to a priest, who had said that, to receive absolution, he would have to give her up. He had replied, 'I must find another confessor,' an exchange he used in his novel *The Heart of the Matter*. They had much in common, as she represented an identical mixture of carnality and Catholicism.

Despite Greene's pleas, at the height of their affair, she proved unwilling to abandon Walston, as she valued both his kindness and the fabulously comfortable lifestyle that went with marriage to him. Also, she must have suspected that Greene was better kept as a lover than a husband.

Greene lived on the 'wrong' north side of Clapham Common, and his house there had been bombed in the war. *The End of the Affair* explores the triangular relationships between an up and coming writer, Bendrix, his lover, Sarah, and her husband, Henry. Sarah and Henry live on the more fashionable south side of the Common. Bendrix is frustrated by Sarah's unwillingness to divorce her boring but amiable husband. Sarah is told that her lover's house has been bombed and he is missing. She makes a vow to God that if he is found alive, she will end the affair. When he survives, she does. As he tries to win her back, she falls ill from a lung infection and dies. Bendrix prays to God to simply leave him alone for ever as love is too painful.

In 1955, the novel, hailed by Evelyn Waugh and many others as a masterpiece, was made into a very popular film, with Deborah Kerr as Sarah. A further successful film version was made in 1999, with Julianne Moore as Sarah and Ralph Fiennes as Bendrix.

Their affair had cooled by the time Greene published the book, though it continued sporadically until 1966, when Greene moved to

Antibes to enjoy his liaison with Yvonne Cloetta, to the annoyance of her husband, until close to his death in 1991.

* * *

In 1939, sandwiched between his far more powerful *Brighton Rock* and *The Heart of the Matter*, Greene had published his first quasi spy story, *The Confidential Agent*. To earn some money and avoid distraction, this was written by him, fuelled with Benzedrine, in six weeks in a flat he rented in Bloomsbury, though he did find time to have an affair with the landlady's daughter.

The story is that of 'D', a distinguished professor from a European country coming to Britain to persuade an English tycoon, Lord Benditch, to supply a large amount of coal to help his government, which is enmeshed in a war against right wing rebels (as was the case in Spain at the time). He befriends Rose, the estranged daughter of Benditch, but is attacked by an English supporter of the rebels. After further misadventures, his mission ends in failure. Benditch decides against selling coal to the rebels, but 'D' ends up with Rose.

Greene was so dissatisfied with the novel that he wanted it published anonymously. The *New York Times* declared it a tour de force, but readers declined to agree. Set in England, it was entirely lacking in the powerful atmospherics of his future espionage novels set in Vienna, Saigon and Havana. An altered version, with Charles Boyer as 'D' and Lauren Bacall as Rose, was turned into a film in 1945. Bacall begged not to have to make it and the film did not thrive.

In 1949, Greene wrote not a full book but a novella that, he declared later, was not intended to be read but to be seen. He started simply with the idea of attending the funeral of a man, who he then sees walking past him 'without a sign of recognition, amidst a host of strangers in the Strand'. It was the film producer, Alexander Korda, who asked him to write a film for the director, Carol Reed, to be set in Vienna.

The film script, written with the input at every stage of Carol Reed, was described by Graham Greene as the finished version of his novel, which he titled *The Third Man*. It was Orson Welles who injected into the script, 'In Switzerland, they had brotherly love, they had five hundred years of democracy and peace, and what did that produce? The cuckoo clock.'

In an unforgettable portrait of a seedy, corrupt and broken down Vienna under allied occupation at the end of the war, the narrator is a British police officer, Calloway. He and his assistant, Sergeant Paine, are investigating the criminal activities of Harry Lime. Holly Martins, a writer of Western novels and a childhood friend of Lime, has been invited to visit him in Vienna to see his work with war refugees there.

On arrival in Vienna, he is told that Lime has been killed in a car accident. But, attending the funeral, he hears different accounts of what happened. Two men were reported to have carried him from the scene, but the porter at Lime's apartment talked of a 'third man' being present at Lime's death. The porter is killed before Martins can see him again. Martins asks for help from Lime's girlfriend, Anna, with whom he has fallen in love. Calloway tells Martins that Lime was stealing penicillin from military hospitals, diluting it and selling it on the black market, injuring or killing countless children.

Martins plans to leave. But after leaving Anna's apartment that evening, he notices her cat and someone watching him from a doorway. He recognises and calls out to Lime, who vanishes into the Vienna sewers. The British police exhume Lime's coffin, finding in it the body of the missing orderly who stole the penicillin for him. Martins, meeting Lime for a ride on the Vienna light railway, is threatened by him. Calloway asks for his help to arrest Lime. Martins agrees, if Calloway will protect Anna, who fears deportation to the Soviet sector, but she wants no part in any action against Lime.

Martins again plans to leave Vienna, but Calloway shows him children whose lives have been ruined by Lime's diluted penicillin, so Martins agrees to help the police. He meets Lime in a cafe, but Lime is warned by Anna. To get away, Lime shoots and kills Paine, but Calloway badly wounds him. Lime drags himself up a stairway to a street grating but cannot raise it. Martins finds Lime, with Calloway shouting at him to shoot him. Lime and Martins exchange looks, before Martins shoots him with Paine's pistol.

Greene had intended a positive ending, with Anna, after her long walk from the grave of Harry Lime, leaving with Martins, but he was overruled by Carol Reed, who proved to be 'triumphantly right', in insisting instead on Anna (Alida Valli) walking straight past Martins without even looking at him – a far more powerful ending.

The film, with Orson Welles in one of his greatest roles as Harry Lime, has been hailed ever since as one of the greatest British movies ever made. Reed captured the bleak and crime ridden atmosphere of post war Vienna by shooting it entirely in black and white, with a host of unusual camera angles. Reed and the cast of the film discovered Anton Karas playing his zither in a Viennese bistro. Reed turned what became known as the haunting 'Harry Lime Theme' into the musical background of the entire film, making it a No. 1 bestseller.

In his next spy story, *The Quiet American*, published in 1955, the narrator, Fowler, is an experienced and disillusioned journalist covering the war between the French and the communists in Vietnam, using Greene's experience as a war correspondent there between 1951 and 1954. No one has captured more vividly the atmosphere of danger, laced with excitement, prevailing in Saigon in wartime. Fowler loves his beautiful, apparently fragile Vietnamese girlfriend Phuong. Otherwise, his mantra is *not to get involved*. He is friends with the equally hard boiled French police chief, Vigot. Riding on a French warplane, he sees it shoot up a *sampan* on the Mekong with no way of knowing if any enemy were involved. The pilot tells him that he knows the French are going to lose the war, but he still has to carry out his duty to keep fighting.

A brash, young new American arrival, Pyle, tries to befriend Fowler. He claims to be part of the aid mission but clearly is there for other reasons. He arrives certain that the solution to Vietnam's problems lies not with the government or the communists, but in the creation of a 'third force' (which was a fashionable notion at the time). He falls heavily for Phuong and is regarded by her sister as a better bet for her than Fowler. When Pyle and Fowler venture into a war zone, a communist Viet Minh attack on a guard tower leaves Fowler injured and Pyle saves his life. Back in Saigon, Fowler lies to Phuong that his wife has agreed to divorce him. His lie is exposed and Phuong moves in with Pyle. Fowler cannot bear the thought of this beautiful creature being turned into an American housewife. Pyle, he comments, is making him hostile to all things American – a near constant theme with Greene.

A car bomb in Saigon kills a lot of innocent people – apparently as part of a plot to make a local warlord, General Thé, head of the 'third force'. Fowler discovers that Pyle provided the explosives; Vigot also knows this. The communists, who are blamed for the explosion, ask Fowler to help them kill Pyle, which he does by inviting him to his apartment and signalling to them when he leaves. He gets back together with Phuong, who reacts impassively to Pyle's disappearance. Not so fragile after all, she seems more like a human embodiment of her country at war.

The novel was a major success, initially due to the authenticity of Greene's descriptions of life in Saigon. As the war was taken over from the French by the Americans, his novel came increasingly to be seen as prophetic about the inability of the US to apply its 'exceptionalism' to Vietnam. It was made into a film in 1958, with Michael Redgrave as Fowler and Audie Murphy as Pyle. But, to Greene's disgust, to appeal to American audiences at the time, the director, Joseph Mankiewicz, with input from the CIA agent, Edward Lansdale, turned the novel on its head, so instead of a warning about external involvement, its message was the need to defeat the communists.

In the 1960s, as the US got bogged down in Vietnam, the novel became cult reading on American campuses. In 2002, a further film was produced, to critical acclaim, with the original ending and Michael Caine as Fowler.

But unlike John le Carré, who concentrated on the tragic dimensions of espionage, Greene enjoyed depicting its sometimes hilarious and absurd dimension too. In 1957, together with his brother, Hugh, Graham Greene published *The Spy's Bedside Book*, consisting of short extracts from their favourite spy stories. Tongues in cheek, they dedicated it to 'the immortal memory' of the melo-dramatic William Le Queux, as well as to John Buchan. Sales were helped, it was alleged, by the East German Secret Service ordering a hundred copies!

In his introduction, Greene enquired if John Buchan's opening to *Greenmantle*, 'A Mission is Proposed,' did not sound more realistic than the actual account by the valet 'Cicero' of his visit to the German Embassy to offer to spy on the British Ambassador in Turkey. Also stranger than fiction was the butterfly net used by Baden-Powell to disguise his spying on fortifications in the Mediterranean. Bond's equipment imagined by Ian Fleming was 'certainly no more fantastic' than the actual furnishings, including machine guns trained on all visitors, in the 'well appointed office' of Walter Schellenberg of the German Secret Service, who also carried suicide pills both in a false tooth and in a signet ring for use if he were captured while travelling abroad.

The last of Greene's spy novels followed in 1958. Greene loved the louche atmosphere of Havana, with its brothels, casinos and out of control nightlife, 'where every vice was permissible and every trade possible', spending a lot of his time there in the 1950s. *Our Man in Havana* was his only unashamedly comic novel, having fun at the expense of all intelligence services, especially MI6. It too was embellished by his absorption of the atmosphere and what he described as the corrupt essence of Havana in the last years of the authoritarian Batista regime.

James Wormold, in Havana as a vacuum cleaner salesman, is

approached by Hawthorne to become an agent for MI6. Wormold's wife has left him and he lives with his beautiful teenage daughter, Millie, who is Catholic but capricious, with expensive tastes. Wormold accepts the offer to help to pay for Millie's would be lifestyle. As he has no information worth reporting, he fabricates reports based on the local newspapers (a frequent sin among intelligence agents) and invents a supposed network of agents. Some of his 'contacts' are real people he has never met; others are simply made up. Wormold tells his friend and war veteran, Dr Hasselbacher, about his activities but not Millie.

To make his reports more exciting, he reports the existence of a secret weapons installation in the mountains, accompanied by scaled up pictures of vacuum cleaner parts. Hawthorne, who knows Wormold's occupation, is sceptical about his report but dares not say so for fear of losing his job. London sends Wormold a secretary and radio assistant, Beatrice. Beatrice has orders to take over Wormold's contacts, starting with his fictitious informant, a pilot called 'Raúl'. But before she can do so, a real Raúl is killed in an apparent car accident. Threats are made to his other contacts, with Beatrice still believing that they are real informants and Wormold trying to save them.

London warns Wormold that an attempt will be made to poison him at a trade association event. When he gets there, Dr Hasselbacher also loudly warns him. He refuses the meal that is served, but a rival vacuum cleaner salesman called Carter offers him a whisky. Wormold knocks over the glass; the contents kill a dog that laps them up and Carter kills Dr Hasselbacher.

A military commander, Captain Segura, claims to have a list of all the spies in Havana. To redeem himself, Wormold tries to get hold of this through a game of draughts played with miniature bottles of Scotch, which have to be drunk immediately a piece is taken. Though a far better player, Segura falls into a drunken stupor. Wormold records the list with a microdot camera, but when processed, the microdot turns out to be blank. During a visit to a local brothel, he manages to shoot Carter. Segura orders him out of Cuba. He confesses to Beatrice, who seems quite impressed by his exploits.

Summoned back to headquarters, to avoid embarrassment and prevent him talking to the press, Wormold is offered a teaching post by MI6 and recommended for the Order of the British Empire. He marries Beatrice and sends Millie to a Swiss finishing school with his proceeds.

In October 1958, after researching in Havana locales for a film version, Greene wrote to the Labour Party MP Hugh Delargy, asking him to table a parliamentary question about continuing British arms sales to Cuba under Batista. The head of the American Department in the Foreign Office, who did not believe that Castro would come to power 'in the foreseeable future', favoured continuing them. After a stormy debate triggered by Greene's letter, the government agreed to halt arms exports. Castro's rebels captured Havana in January 1959.

In April, Greene and the director, Carol Reed, returned to Havana to work on the film. Castro, now in power, agreed that it could be made there but complained that the novel had not adequately portrayed the brutality of the Batista regime, which Greene accepted. The film must also show the new regime 'in the right light', causing Reed to have to make numerous, though not very important, changes to the script.

The outcome was a remarkable film, superbly directed by Carol

Reed, with Alec Guinness as Wormold and Noël Coward as Hawthorne. Castro was pictured on the set with Alec Guinness and Maureen O'Hara. In a later, new introduction to *Our Man in Havana*, Greene described having travelled to Santiago de Cuba, still under Batista, with a consignment of warm clothes for Castro's men, which he handed over in a safe house there.

Greene was an ardent, uncritical admirer of Castro as the epitome of the sort of charismatic, revolutionary, anti-American leader he admired. When Gabriel García Márquez asked him, in Castro's presence, whether he really had played Russian roulette with a loaded gun, Greene told him that he had done so multiple times, with both Castro and Márquez surprised that, in that case, he should still be alive. Márquez became for a while an official in Castro's government. Greene met him twice and had numerous meetings with other key members of the regime as, in the 1960s, he became Castro's best known and unconditional apologist and propagandist.

'There is an extraordinarily likeable quality about the man,' he declared, contending that history would have been different if Eisenhower had not been 'too busy playing golf' to meet him. In Greene's later apartment in Antibes, pride of place went to a picture by a Cuban artist that Castro had given him and signed on the back, causing him 'not to know which way round to hang it'.

In 1976, Greene was summoned to meet General Torrijos, de facto ruler of Panama from 1968 to 1981, for whom he developed a similar political infatuation, which he recorded in his *Getting to Know the General*. Torrijos came to power in a *coup d'état* against the moderate civilian President Arias. He was never formally President of Panama, describing himself instead as 'Maximum Leader of the

Panamanian Revolution'. Greene supported Torrijos's successful negotiation of new treaties with the US, leading to eventual Panamanian control of the Canal and Canal Zone, though President Carter warned him that the new treaties would not be ratified until some form of democracy was restored in Panama.

Greene also was impressed by the fact that, as a populist, Torrijos was looking to win the support of the mainly native or mixed heritage poor against the white elite of Spanish descent. He opened many new schools and prosecuted oligarchs. His most popular measure was the redistribution of land from major landowners and US multinationals to peasant farmers. Márquez also was a supporter of Torrijos.

Flattered by his attention, Greene made four visits to Panama for lengthy, alcohol fuelled meetings with Torrijos, whom he described as exhibiting 'the charisma of near despair'. He was due to make a fifth when Torrijos was killed in a plane crash. Through Torrijos, Greene also met the communist *sandinista* leaders from Nicaragua. Torrijos, however, was becoming disillusioned with Castro and the *sandinistas*; he was wary of the Soviets and did not want to burn all his bridges with the US.

* * *

Graham Greene had long been a communist sympathiser, though never, except briefly at Oxford, a party member.

Nevertheless, it came as a surprise when he rallied to the defence of his former mentor in MI6, Kim Philby. For when Philby published in 1968 his rationale for his treachery in *My Silent War*, his book carried with it an exculpatory introduction by Graham

Greene, presenting the case for betrayal as part of the human condition, which could in the end be forgiven. None of Philby's other former colleagues were in a forgiving mood since, as well as betraying secrets, Philby had been responsible for the deaths of a large number of anti-communists despatched to Albania in operations for which, with the Americans, he was directly in charge. He was, in their opinion, a murderer.

Undeterred, Greene, who enjoyed scandalising people, wrote,

> The end, of course, in his eyes, is held to justify the means, but this is a view taken, perhaps less openly, by most men in politics ... He betrayed his country – yes, perhaps he did, but who among us has not committed treason to something or someone more important than a country?

Philby had displayed the same 'chilling certainty' as the Catholics who worked for the Spanish under Elizabeth I. It was the 'logical fanaticism of a man who, once having found a faith, is not going to lose it because of the cruelties or injustices inflicted by erring human instruments'. Greene, in another instance, declared that Philby 'was serving a cause, not himself, and so my old liking for him came back.' He followed this up by giving a speech in Hamburg entitled, 'The Virtue of Disloyalty.'

Although thereafter he communicated regularly with Philby, the reactions to his introduction seemed to deter him from seeking an early meeting. But in 1986, Greene was invited to Moscow by the Soviet Writers' Union, affording the opportunity for a meeting with Philby and his Russian wife, Rufina. Philby wrote to say that the three days they had spent together were among the happiest in

Rufina's life. Greene's partner, Yvonne Cloetta, who also was present, described Philby as 'the one man for whom Graham committed himself utterly'. Five months later, Greene made a further visit to Moscow. Rufina described the two old friends embracing each other and reminiscing, laughing and joking together over lashings of vodka.

CHAPTER X

THE CAMBRIDGE SPIES

The story of the Cambridge 'Ring of Five' Soviet spies begins not with them but with their inspired recruiter, Arnold Deutsch. Probably of Czech origin, Deutsch earned a doctorate from the University of Vienna then secured a postgraduate post at the University of London, having been an active agent of the Comintern (Communist International) from his student days. For Deutsch it was who came up with a strategy to recruit, protect and implant high level Soviet agents in key parts of the British system. It was based on his observation, as a fellow academic, that many idealistic young students at Cambridge were attracted by Marxist ideas of a, supposedly, more just and equal society and the conviction that the communists were the most effective adversaries of fascism. He also observed that a high proportion of the senior positions in the Foreign Office and intelligence services were filled by Cambridge graduates. So, the objective should be to attract some of the best and brightest of susceptible new graduates and then persuade them to act swiftly to mask their interest in communism as merely a student aberration. They then should be instructed to apply to enter the most sensitive areas of the British system.

Deutsch was the most effective recruiter of high level spies the Soviets ever had, until he left Britain in 1937. Philby rhapsodised about his extraordinary humanistic qualities. In 1940, he disappeared. Reassigned to the Americas, he was believed to have been aboard the *Donbass* when it was torpedoed by a German U-boat.

Born in India in 1912, Philby was christened Harold but nicknamed 'Kim', after Kipling's youthful hero, by his father, the distinguished Arabist St John Philby. While studying at Trinity College, Cambridge, he displayed a 'leaning towards communism'. Maurice Dobb, teaching Marxist economics and a member of the Communist Party, had quite a following in Cambridge. Dobb, who was Philby's economics tutor, introduced Philby to a German anti-fascist communist front organisation. In 1934, Philby married a young German communist, Litzi Friedmann. She introduced him to a new experience, that of making love in the snow. 'Not as cold as you would expect, once you get used to it,' was Philby's comment. She told him that she was arranging for him a meeting 'of decisive importance'.

On 1 July that year, at a meeting in Regent's Park, he was introduced by her to Arnold Deutsch, who recruited him as a Soviet agent. Deutsch told him that he must break off all communist contacts. He should try to establish a new political image as a right wing, even fascist sympathiser. 'He must become, to all outward appearances, a conventional member of the very class he was committed to opposing … The anti-fascist movement needs people who can enter into the bourgeoisie.'

Philby recommended to Deutsch several of his Cambridge contemporaries, including Donald Maclean and Guy Burgess, despite his reservations about Burgess's erratic personality. They were recruited by Deutsch in the same year. All three were members of the Cambridge University Socialist Society, which at the time was a communist front organisation. As instructed, they then began quickly to cover their tracks, with Burgess shocking his friends by becoming stridently anti-communist. (Illustrating the overlap at the time between Marxist true believers and the 'establishment', Guy Burgess's brother, Nigel, joined MI5, as did Donald Maclean's sister, Nancy, while Philby's sister, Helena, worked for MI6.)

By 1936, Philby and Friedmann had separated, though Philby brought her to Britain when the Germans were about to overrun Paris in 1940. Litzi was extremely well known in European communist circles but not to the British authorities, who showed no interest in her. They did not divorce until 1946.

Philby became editor of the failing *Anglo-Russian Trade Gazette*, which was diverted by its owner to cover Anglo-German trade. He also became a member of the Anglo-German Fellowship, set up to promote friendly relations with Germany, enabling him to make frequent visits to Berlin. In February 1937, he moved to Spain to cover the Spanish Civil War, initially as a freelance journalist. His move there was financed by Soviet intelligence. By May, he had been hired to cover the conflict by *The Times*, reporting from the headquarters of the pro-Franco forces in Seville. He communicated with his Soviet controllers via letters to a Mlle Dupont at an address he subsequently was alarmed to discover was that of the Soviet Embassy in Paris.

By this time, he also was sending reports to MI6, who wanted estimates of the strength of Franco's forces. Reports to them were sent via the British Embassy in Paris. Philby's NKVD controller in Paris, a Latvian called Ozolin-Haskins (code name Pierre) was shot in Stalin's purges. Two years later, the same happened to his next controller, Boris Bazarov.

He picked up some useful intelligence. For Philby was able to report to MI6 that Franco had told him that German troops would not be permitted to cross Spain to attack Gibraltar. Both the British and the Soviets were looking for information on the performance of the Messerschmitts and German Panzers deployed with Franco.

By May 1937, his new and far more senior Soviet controller Theodore Maly was investigating the possibility of assassinating Franco, but he reported to the NKVD that Philby, 'though devoted and ready to sacrifice himself ... does not possess the physical courage necessary' for such an attempt. In December, a car in which Philby was travelling with other correspondents was hit by shelling from the Republican lines. The others were killed, but Philby suffered only minor injuries. It was for this incident that, in March 1938, Franco presented Philby with the Red Cross of Military Merit. The fact that he had been decorated by Franco served as a huge advertisement for his supposed anti-communist credentials. In 1939, Philby returned to *The Times*. He reported on the British Expeditionary Force's evacuation from Dunkirk and the fall of France.

Donald Maclean was known to be a communist by his

contemporaries at Cambridge. Having earned first class honours in modern languages, urged on by Deutsch, he applied to join the Foreign Office. In the entrance exam, he was asked whether he had favoured communism as a student. He was able to get away with, 'I was initially favourable to it, but I am little by little getting disenchanted with it.'

The Eton educated Guy Burgess was a very well connected socialite. Burgess and Anthony Blunt became accustomed to staying in Lord Victor Rothschild's flat in London. Having flourished as a BBC editor and producer, he was recruited also by MI6 on the usual 'old boy' basis, with no vetting. He was blatantly homosexual at a time when that was still frowned upon. He also had an ever worsening drinking problem, plus slovenly personal habits, none of which prevented him getting a post in the News Department of the Foreign Office.

In 1940, it was on the recommendation of Burgess that Philby, with no vetting and checks on his past whatever, joined MI6, serving in what he regarded as the 'tiny, ineffective and slightly comic' Section D (for Destruction!), where he and Burgess were supposed to train agents in sabotage. Burgess was arrested for drunk driving and fired, but Philby continued as an instructor. His Soviet handlers refused to believe that this chaotically amateurish operation could actually be part of the real MI6; he was urged to penetrate deeper.

In 1940, a Soviet GRU defector, Walter Krivitsky, told MI5 that two Soviet agents had penetrated the British Foreign Office and a third had worked as a journalist for a British newspaper in Spain. Philby's controller in Madrid, Alexander Orlov, also defected, but to protect his family in Russia, he kept quiet about Philby. Philby, meanwhile, tried unsuccessfully to recruit as a Soviet agent Flora Solomon, who had been a girlfriend of Kerensky who, for just three months, had been Prime Minister of Russia, before the Bolsheviks took over.

But Theodore Maly, by then his controller, told Moscow that he was still suspicious about Philby's motives. The new KGB London resident Ivan Chichayev (code name 'Vadim') asked Philby for a list of British agents being trained to enter the Soviet Union. Philby replied that none had been sent or were being trained. This was underlined in red in the KGB archives, with two question marks, registering their disbelief and doubts about Philby, who warned his contacts of the impending German attack, as did Churchill to a disbelieving Stalin.

Elena Modrzhinskaya, who assessed for the KGB all the material from the Cambridge Five, was deeply suspicious about Philby's failure to report anti-communist activities. Also, she wanted to know, 'Could the SIS really be such fools that they failed to notice suitcase loads of documents leaving the office? How could they have overlooked Philby's communist wife?' She concluded that the Five were double agents, working for MI6. Yuri Modin, controller of the Cambridge spies from 1948 to 1951, also initially suspected, even at that stage, that they might be double agents.

From September 1941, Philby had been working for Section Five of MI6, responsible for counter-intelligence. Given his knowledge of Spain, he was tasked with seeking to neutralise the efforts of German military intelligence (the Abwehr) there and in Portugal and since the British could access Abwehr codes, he proved very effective in doing so. His agents uncovered German plans to establish a listening post in Algeciras to monitor all traffic to and from Gibraltar and through the Straits. He recommended that the ambassador, Sir Samuel Hoare, should protest direct to Franco, which the ambassador, in full regalia, proceeded to do. The Germans were obliged hastily to cancel the operation.

Philby by this time had been promoted to be deputy head of the section under a former senior Indian police officer, Felix Cowgill. He had learned to have a healthy respect for MI5, as the German agents in Britain had been rounded up in short order at the beginning of the war. He found MI5 to be far more professionally staffed and organised than the improvised mix of people in MI6. He was especially impressed by the deputy head Guy Liddell, who later was accused, wrongly, of being a Soviet agent.

By 1944, as it was clear that the Soviet Union could pose a serious post war threat to Britain, MI6 reactivated Section Nine to concert all anti-communist activities. His Soviet controllers insisted that Philby must stop at nothing to take over from Cowgill. As Cowgill was on poor terms with MI5, the Foreign Office and the deputy head of SIS, who considered Philby to be more user friendly and modern minded, campaigned successfully to promote him. When Philby was appointed head of Section Nine, he insisted that MI5 must also approve, which they did. When a furious Cowgill resigned, Sections Nine and Five were merged. So the overall head of counter-intelligence for SIS, including vis-à-vis the Soviet Union, now was a Soviet spy.

He enjoyed some private jokes at his colleagues' expense, keeping in his office a picture of Mount Ararat – from the Soviet side.

While never, of course, admitting to the numerous follies of the KGB, including doubting his own intelligence reports, Philby enjoyed telling stories about the shortcomings of some of his SIS colleagues. As, by the end of 1943, there was a trickle of German defectors, British missions overseas were warned to treat them with suspicion and not to give them any commitments without approval from headquarters. When an officer in the German Foreign Ministry with a briefcase full of documents appeared at the British Legation in Berne, he was chased away by the military attaché and the head of chancery. So he tried the US legation, where his documents were accepted with enthusiasm by Allen Dulles, whose first major intelligence coup this was. The senior SIS officer dealing with Switzerland, Claude Dansey, resented Dulles and the Americans' arrival on 'his' territory. He dismissed the documents as an obvious plant without even reading them.

As the Americans shared them with the British, Philby did read them and checked them with the British cryptographers, who pronounced them genuine. In Dansey's absence, he distributed them to the Foreign Office and Ministry of Defence, who cried out for more. Summoned by an irate Dansey, Philby pointed out that he had distributed them not as US but as 'our' intelligence, causing Dansey to conclude, 'You're not such a fool as I thought!'

This episode, while embarrassing, does not exactly rank with Stalin's refusal to believe Churchill's warning that Germany was about to invade Russia.

The counter-intelligence section of SIS included the in house expert on communism, Bob Carew Hunt, who had to be dissuaded from dedicating his work on *The Theory and Practice of Communism* to Philby! It also included Jane Archer, who, while in MI5, had been warned by the Soviet defector Krivitsky about a British journalist in Spain, but showed no sign of making the connection.

In August 1945, an NKVD agent in Istanbul, Konstantin Volkov, asked the British Consulate there for political asylum in Britain. For a large payment, he offered to name three Soviet agents, two of whom worked in the Foreign Office, the third in counter-intelligence in London. For Philby, this turned out, as he put it, to be 'a very narrow squeak indeed'. For, initially, Sir Stewart Menzies, still head of SIS, assigned an MI5 officer, Brigadier Roberts, to go to Istanbul. But Roberts had a phobia about flying, so Philby was able to volunteer to do so himself.

Philby alerted the Soviets and helped to engineer enough delays to give them three weeks to deal with Volkov before he arrived in Istanbul, ostensibly to see him. Volkov was last seen, heavily band-aged, being bundled aboard a Soviet plane to Moscow. Officials in the consulate were appalled at the delay in responding. Philby contended that the Soviets must have intercepted the embassy's or Volkov's phone communications or have had their own suspicions about him. Yet, incredibly, he was never called to account for the three weeks' delay in trying to see him. As for sending Volkov to his death, he appeared to have no regrets about that whatsoever.

After a period as head of the MI6 station in Turkey, in September 1949, he was appointed as the head of MI6 in Washington, in charge of liaison with the Americans on all intelligence matters. There, he resumed contact with James Angleton, who he knew already from Angleton's service in the US Embassy in London. Angleton claimed subsequently to have had suspicions about Philby, but at the time, he exchanged innumerable confidences with him over their weekly lunches at a restaurant called Harvey's.

In Albania, Colonel David Smiley of the Special Air Service (SAS) had helped Enver Hoxha and the communists to liberate their country from the Germans. That achieved, Smiley then hoped to organise a rebellion by the anti-communist supporters of the exiled King Zog to oust Hoxha. From 1947, some insurgent groups were infiltrated successfully into Albania overland from Greece. The then head of MI6, Sir Stewart Menzies, disliked this venture, considering it to be more fitting for special operations than for an intelligence organisation. From 1948, it increasingly was taken over by the newly formed CIA, with the gung-ho Frank Wisner especially keen on it and larger groups were landed by sea and air. As the UK representative, Philby was co-chairman of the committee overseeing the operation, enabling him to betray all the planned landings. Many of those despatched were killed; others imprisoned.

Philby wrote subsequently that

the agents we sent into Albania were armed men intent on murder, sabotage and assassination … They knew the risks they were running. I was serving the interests of the Soviet Union and those interests required that these men were defeated. To the extent that I helped to defeat them, even if it caused their deaths, I have no regrets.

He also betrayed the landings of some small groups of anti-communists in Ukraine.

Before leaving for Washington, Philby was briefed on the 'Venona' intercepts of Soviet intelligence communications, thereby revealing the programme to the Soviets, though too late for them to undo the damage. He was told that the intercepts revealed the existence of a British spy in the Manhattan Project at Los Alamos and of one who had served in the British Embassy in Washington, code named 'Homer'.

CHAPTER XI

PHILBY AND THE ART OF GETTING AWAY WITH TREASON

Kim Philby, once installed in Moscow, explained in his tenden-tious but illuminating memoir, *My Silent War*, precisely how he had planned and managed to use the British system of justice to avoid any retribution for his treachery.

At the end of 1949, the atom spy was identified as Dr Klaus Fuchs. On his return to Britain, he was arrested and interrogat-ed by William Skardon of MI5. Philby had no connection with Fuchs, but to his dismay, Skardon had been so successful in winning Fuchs's confidence that Fuchs not only confessed to being a Soviet agent himself, but he also incriminated the courier, Harry Gold and, through him, Julius and Ethel Rosenberg. In Philby's mind, this reinforced the lesson he had been taught by Arnold Deutsch: never confess.

In the summer of 1950, Philby received a letter from Guy Burgess.

'I have a surprise for you,' it said. 'I have just been posted to Washington.' He hoped that he could stay with Philby. Philby could hardly refuse since, as he said, he had recommended Burgess for recruitment by the Soviets and Burgess had recommended him to MI6. Also, he knew that Burgess was 'very apt to get into personal scrapes of a spectacular nature'. The embassy were warned of this by the Foreign Office, with details of Burgess's past scandals and expressing concern that worse might follow. Philby records that the embassy security officer, reading this, wondered what 'worse' might mean. 'Goats?' he speculated.

Burgess had reached the peak of his effectiveness as a Soviet spy when, from 1945 to 1950, he served in the office of Hector McNeil, deputy to the Foreign Secretary, Ernest Bevin. Nearly all of the important documents intended for Bevin were copied to McNeil. Thanks to absurdly lax document security, Burgess was able to send to Moscow several thousand documents ranging from confidential to top secret, including about the plans for the formation of NATO.

Burgess lived in constant fear of exposure as he had tried to recruit the journalist Goronwy Rees as a Soviet agent and feared that he would be denounced by him. He even suggested to his controller that the Soviets should consider assassinating Rees, an idea they did not take seriously. He was a chronic alcoholic and a promiscuous homosexual. Frequently dishevelled and the worse for wear, trouble followed him everywhere. He was quite badly injured when an exasperated fellow member pushed him down the steps of the Garrick Club. According to Philby, there also had been problems in Dublin and Tangier. The KGB by this time were disillusioned with Burgess as he was 'constantly drunk'.

So Philby agreed that Burgess could stay with him, in the hope of keeping him under some control. But Burgess, who was virulently anti-American, lost no time antagonising as many Americans as he could. One drunken evening, he triggered a furious row and near fist fight with Bill Harvey, a key deputy of J. Edgar Hoover, by drawing a lewd cartoon of Harvey's wife. The FBI also had protested about him 'cruising' through Arlington in his embassy car in search of male company.

Before leaving for Washington, Philby was told that one of those suspected of being the Soviet spy 'Homer' was his fellow Cambridge spy, Donald Maclean.

In 1937, having finished work in the Foreign Office, Maclean would head in the evenings to the flat in Bayswater of Kitty Harris, wife of the leader of the US Communist Party. Over the next two years, forty-five boxes of documents were photographed and sent to Moscow.

On being posted as a First Secretary in the British Embassy in Washington, Maclean came to be regarded as a rising star in the Foreign Service. He was described by his colleague Robert Cecil as the hardest working member of the ambassador's staff. He then was posted on promotion to Cairo, as the youngest counsellor in the Foreign Service.

Once there, he experienced some difficulty in communicating material to his Soviet contacts. His American wife, Melinda, was a wholehearted collaborator in his spying. She solved the problem by booking appointments at the hairdresser at the same time as the Soviet Ambassador's wife and passing documents to her. By this time, the strain of his double life was taking its toll on Maclean. In a drunken episode, he trashed the flat of a secretary in the US

Embassy. His wife told the Foreign Office that he needed to be recalled to London for medical reasons.

Despite this background, after a period of rehabilitation, he was appointed head of the American Department of the Foreign Office, giving him access to nearly all material on Anglo-American relations, enabling him to send a further flood of secret and confidential material to Moscow. This included confirming the British intention to develop nuclear weapons, though, unlike Klaus Fuchs, he couldn't provide any technical information.

Burgess, having antagonised a host of Americans by his drunken and boorish behaviour, was on the verge of having to resign or being dismissed anyway. As the net by now was closing around 'Homer', Philby needed to send him back to London to warn Maclean. So, in early May 1951, Burgess broke the speed limit in Virginia three times in one day, causing the Governor to insist on his recall. When he left, Philby hastened to bury Burgess's radio transmitter and other spy paraphernalia in a nearby wood. Philby's instructions to Burgess were, 'Don't you go too,' as that would leave Philby exposed.

Burgess duly warned Maclean in a meeting at his club but not with sufficient urgency. Knowing that Maclean was due to be interrogated on 28 May, on 23 May, Philby sent Burgess a coded message, ostensibly about his Lincoln convertible in the embassy car park that 'if he did not act at once, it would be too late'.

Moscow Centre and Yuri Modin had decided that Maclean must be extracted, as he was in such a state that he would break down under interrogation. Burgess at first resisted, but Modin told him that he must leave with Maclean, the centre having concluded that 'we had not just one burnt out agent, but two'.

On the 25th, Burgess drove Maclean from his house in Surrey to

Southampton, where they caught the ferry to St Malo. Although the suspicions about him by now were red hot, Maclean had not been placed under any effective surveillance. On being informed that Burgess had absconded as well as Maclean, as Philby put it, 'his consternation was no pretence' for, in explaining their defection, this put him squarely in the firing line.

His first task was to inform the FBI of their disappearance. As, clearly, he would very shortly be summoned back to London and interrogated, he tried to estimate his chances of survival, rating them as quite good. His left wing associations at Cambridge were well known, but he had never actually joined the Communist Party. The Soviet defector Krivitsky had mentioned a British journalist who had gone to Spain, but others had done so at the time. There was the awkward fact that Burgess had recommended him to MI6. It would have been pretty fatal if the security service had checked all the files he had taken out to photograph, but the records were not well kept. Nevertheless, in view of episodes like the Volkov case and his foreknowledge of the action about to be taken against Maclean, he was faced with the 'inescapable conclusion' that he could not hope to prove his innocence.

But that did not mean that all was lost. Given his knowledge of the English legal system, Philby was confident that all the circumstantial evidence against him would not be sufficient to convict him *so long as he did not confess anything*, which he had no intention of doing. What also should help him, he calculated, was that plenty of senior figures, especially in MI6, would be seriously embarrassed if it turned out that, all along, he had been a Soviet spy.

The Americans, he realised, were liable to prove more difficult. He had a low opinion of Hoover and Dulles but not of General

Bedell Smith, head of the CIA who 'had a cold, fishy eye and a precision tool brain'. He would be liable to 'figure out that two and two made four'.

The Foreign Office had been obliged to describe the two diplomats as 'missing'. It was thought evident that they had decamped to Moscow, but the Soviets did not confirm their presence there until 1956 and, even then, the press agency *TASS* flatly denied that they had ever been spies; they had moved to the Soviet Union 'to further understanding between East and West for the sake of world peace'.

On his recall to London, Philby was summoned forthwith to two meetings with Dick White at MI5, who asked who had paid for his journey to Spain, initially as a freelance reporter. Philby claimed to have done so himself (in reality, the funds had been provided by his Soviet controller, via Burgess).

Philby then was summoned by Sir Hugh Sinclair, the head of MI6, to be told that a very strong letter had been received from General Bedell Smith, ruling out any return by Philby to Washington. A key contributor to this letter had been the Hoover aide insulted by Burgess, Bill Harvey. Harvey had worked out the number of 'coincidences' of things going wrong and Philby's involvement. Sinclair, who believed firmly in Philby's innocence, told him 'with obvious distress' that he would have to ask for Philby's resignation, while promising him a small pension, thereby putting an end to Philby's effective usefulness as a Soviet agent. Thereafter, he was useful mainly for the embarrassment he continued to cause.

Philby then was informed that he would be subject to a 'judicial enquiry' by a well known QC, Helenus 'Buster' Milmo, who had conducted many interrogations for MI5. Philby batted away his questions, but Milmo then produced two unexpected rabbits from his hat. Two days after the Volkov information reached London, there had been a spectacular surge in NKVD wireless traffic between London and Moscow. Then, shortly after Philby had been briefed about the leakage from the embassy in Washington, there had been a similar surge in NKVD traffic. When asked by Milmo 'in his most thunderous tones' how to account for this, Philby said that he had no idea. Fearing that he had indeed been found out, Philby expressed his 'intense anger' about Milmo's interrogation to his most ardent supporter in MI6, Nicholas Elliott.

There followed several more interrogations, conducted with 'exquisite politeness' by William Skardon. This was wasted on Philby, as he knew that it was Skardon who had persuaded Fuchs to confess. Skardon was at least partly taken in by Philby, who made on him a 'more favourable impression' than he had expected. He concluded that the case against him was unproven.

But Milmo, a serious intelligence professional, had not been taken in by Philby at all, and nor had Philby expected him to be. Milmo reported, 'I find myself unable to avoid the conclusion that Philby is and has been for many years a Soviet agent.' But his conclusion also was that the circumstantial evidence was unlikely to be sufficient to secure a conviction in an English court of law.

As to Philby's guilt, that was the conclusion also of Dick White and MI5 but not that of Sir Hugh Sinclair and his colleagues in MI6, who continued to believe that Philby was the victim of unfounded smears and unlucky circumstances.

Nearly four years later, in October 1955, J. Edgar Hoover, unhappy at Philby escaping justice, leaked a story about him as the 'Third

Man' in the New York press. A Labour MP, Marcus Lipton, with contacts in MI5, using parliamentary privilege, asked Sir Anthony Eden 'if he was determined at all costs to cover up the dubious "third man" activities of Mr Harold Philby'. Philby threatened legal action against Lipton, who had to retract his statement when, on 7 November, Harold Macmillan, as Foreign Secretary, in a reply drafted for him by MI6, declared that he had no reason to conclude that Philby had at any time betrayed British interests or to identify him 'as the so called "Third Man", if indeed there was one'. MI5 claimed that they had not been consulted about this enthusiastic exculpation. They would have wanted simply to say 'we do not have evidence' that he was a spy.

Philby gave a triumphant press conference, with no trace of his usual slight stammer, trumpeting his innocence and declaring that 'I have never been a communist'. He claimed that 'the last time I met a communist, knowing that he was one, was in 1934!'

In 1956, MI6 helped Philby to be appointed in Beirut as a correspondent for *The Observer* and *The Economist* and continued to pay him a retainer. In 1961, a KGB Major, Anatoliy Golitsyn, defected to the US. Dick White by then had been appointed head of MI6. Golitsyn confirmed to White his suspicions about Philby. Annoyed by what she regarded as the anti-Israel bias in his press articles, Flora Solomon belatedly told Lord Victor Rothschild that Philby had tried to recruit her as a Soviet spy, though she was not prepared to testify against him.

In January 1963, Philby's close friend and strongest supporter in MI6, Nicholas Elliott, was despatched to Beirut to extract a confession from him. As Philby must have feared exposure by Golitsyn, his drinking had spiralled completely out of control. When Elliott arrived to tell him that the game was up, Philby clearly had been expecting him. Even then, however, according to Philby, Elliott told Philby that 'you stopped working for the Russians in 1949'. This ridiculous assertion was intended to avoid admitting to the Americans that Philby had still been spying when he was the SIS representative in Washington, as of course he was.

In his 'confession', Philby went one better, claiming that he had stopped working for the Soviets since 1946. He had only warned Maclean in 1951 out of personal friendship. The heads of both MI5, Sir Roger Hollis, and even Dick White, now head of MI6, persuaded themselves to believe this nonsense, causing Hollis to write to Hoover one of the silliest and most disgraceful official letters ever to cross the Atlantic. 'In our judgment,' wrote Hollis, Philby's statement was 'substantially true.' They had no evidence of a continuance of his spying efforts after 1946. 'It follows that damage to United States interests will have been confined to the period of the Second World War.'

Hoover and the FBI reacted to this letter with the derision it deserved. It arrived on his desk just one week after Philby fled to Moscow. The official US assessment concluded, correctly, that he had continued spying for the Soviet Union until he was exposed by the defections of Burgess and Maclean in May 1951 and that, as head of the American Department in the Foreign Office, Donald Maclean had access to a vast amount of material of interest to the Soviets. On US/UK atomic energy and the process leading to the establishment of NATO, all the material that had come Maclean's way had ended up in Soviet hands until his defection to Moscow.

As for Philby's pseudo 'confession', when Elliott asked him to sign it, he pleaded for more time. Subsequently, he tried to disavow his statement, even though it was in his handwriting. A further meeting was scheduled for the end of January, with Elliott departing for London.

On 23 January, Philby disappeared from Beirut. The Russian freighter *Dolmatova*, bound for Odessa, left that morning so hurriedly that some of its cargo was left scattered on the docks. In July 1963, the Russians announced that Philby had been granted political asylum and Soviet citizenship.

In his memoir, Philby glosses over his hurried departure. He tries to pretend that he was still of value to his controllers as a journalist in the Middle East, which he clearly wasn't. His nerves by then at last were shot, waiting for the next defector to incriminate him. He assured his KGB controllers, falsely, that he had not made any confession, but they must have feared that, in the next interrogation, Philby would be offered immunity from prosecution in return for a full confession. When he arrived in Moscow, Philby was kept under close surveillance for several years, as the Soviets feared that he might try to return to Britain.

As MI6 were attacked for failing to prevent his defection, Elliott claimed not to have expected this to happen. But even at this stage, there were concerns that he might not be convicted in the British courts. He would argue that his 'confession' had been obtained under duress.

White realised that the last thing Harold Macmillan wanted was the media circus that would have accompanied a public trial. The ability of each of Burgess, Maclean and Philby to photograph and send to Moscow several thousand confidential, secret and top secret documents would have been exposed, together with all the other acts of incompetence that had enabled the three to do so much damage for so long. The trial would have been acutely embarrassing to Macmillan personally, given his earlier 'clearance' of Philby as not being the 'third man, if indeed there was one'. It was for these reasons that Philby himself was convinced that the door had been left wide open for him to defect. His defection saved the reputation of Dick White, who had indeed been supporting offering Philby immunity from prosecution in return for a 'full' confession.

CHAPTER XII

THE 'FOURTH' AND 'FIFTH' MEN

Philby acknowledged that his friend James Angleton, the CIA's head of counter-intelligence, had been close to 'catching on' what he was really up to. The realisation that Philby, plus Burgess and Maclean, had been spies all along reinforced Angleton's conviction that all intelligence agencies, including his own, must be assumed to have been penetrated, as did the allegations of the Soviet defector, Anatoliy Golitsyn, that there was a Soviet 'mole' in a senior position in the CIA. Golitsyn's allegation was discredited, but Angleton's paranoid behaviour remained disruptive within the Agency until he was ousted in 1974.

Much the same happened with a small group led by Peter Wright within MI5. Golitsyn had claimed, and Wright was convinced, that the British Prime Minister, Harold Wilson, was a Soviet spy. Wright also believed that Sir Roger Hollis, head of MI5 from 1956 to 1965, was a Soviet 'mole'. Roger Hollis could not understand why he was being investigated by his own team – unsurprisingly, as the

Soviet archives, when opened, showed no trace of him or other Wright suspects. Roger Hollis, in fact, had suspected that Anthony Blunt was a spy when Wright and co. did not.

Guy Liddell, in charge of counter espionage in MI5, had a very distinguished record. One of his agents, Duško Popov, provided intelligence suggesting that the Japanese might attack Pearl Harbour. Popov was sent to see J. Edgar Hoover, but the FBI did not find him credible. Liddell was scheduled to become head of MI5 but fell under suspicion when his close friend Guy Burgess defected. He also was a friend of Philby and, during the war, had appointed Anthony Blunt as one of his deputies. In response to the MI5 suspicions about Philby, his supporters in MI6 started claiming that that the most likely culprit was not Philby but Liddell. In 1953, following an MI5 internal investigation, he took early retirement.

Liddell was denounced by Goronwy Rees, who had been recruited as a Soviet spy but then broke with them. He was also named as a spy by John Costello in *The Mask of Treachery*. No confirmation was ever found of any betrayal by him. Rupert Allason (Nigel West) concluded that 'his unwise friendships and his preference for homosexual company' had wrecked the reputation of a shrewd intelligence professional.

The spy mania was fuelled dramatically with the publication in 1981 of Chapman Pincher's book *Their Trade is Treachery*. Improbable as it may seem, it was Victor Rothschild, obsessed with the allegations that he too might be a Soviet agent, who bought an air ticket back from Tasmania for Peter Wright so that he could brief Pincher on his activities and the identities of other potential suspects. Rothschild did so knowing that Wright would give effective clearance to him. Pincher's book was devoted mainly to the case against Hollis, which consisted entirely of allegations and no real evidence.

In reality, the 'fourth' man, hiding in plain sight but not firmly identified until 1964, and even then only *in camera*, was Sir Anthony Blunt. Also at Trinity College, Cambridge, he became a close friend and possibly partner (both were homosexual) of Guy Burgess. Burgess had introduced Blunt to Arnold Deutsch, who recruited Blunt, code named 'Tony', in 1937 as a 'talent spotter' for the KGB. Blunt in turn recruited the American Michael Straight and John Cairncross, plus Leo Long, a sub-agent in military intelligence.

Blunt was well known to have had far left associations at Cambridge and to have visited the Soviet Union. He was the only member of the Five to have attracted the early attention of the Security Service, who had disqualified him from joining the Intelligence Corps in 1939. By then, he was 'trying to create the impression that he didn't share left wing views', claiming that he was only interested in the application of Marxism to art history.

None of this prevented him joining MI5 in 1940 on the recommendation of Victor Rothschild to Guy Liddell. Late in 1940, with Liddell's support, he tried to recruit Guy Burgess for MI5 when Burgess was fired from MI6. It was argued that his communist past could make him particularly useful! This was vetoed by another MI5 officer who did not believe that Burgess had abandoned communism.

The KGB archives confirm that between 1941 and 1945, Blunt passed to the Soviets over 1,700 confidential, secret and top secret documents, including intelligence from Ultra transcripts, to the

Soviets. Most of these were viewed with suspicion in Moscow by the redoubtable Elena Modrzhinskaya, as she had heard from Blunt about the Double Cross system employed against German spies and believed that the same technique was being used against Russia. Like Philby, Blunt too had reported that there were no British spies in the Soviet mission in London. 'Not a single valuable British spy in the USSR or in the Soviet Embassy in London had been exposed by the group,' she pointed out. It was inconceivable to her that this was because there weren't any. Yet Soviet military intelligence, the GRU, were very appreciative of the intelligence about German military plans in the battle of Kursk sent to them by Leo Long, asking for more.

From 1943 to 1945, it was Blunt's task to prepare the regular summarised reports to Churchill, marked 'Most Secret' on MI5's activities in the prior month! Presumably, he passed the longer versions of these reports, before they were summarised, to the Soviets.

But the strain of spying had taken such a toll on Blunt that the Soviets did not object when, at the end of the war, he hastened to leave MI5 to join the Courtauld Institute and become Surveyor of the King's Pictures. Thereafter, unlike the other Cambridge spies, he was not very active, apart from reporting items of gossip from his contacts in the intelligence services. For this very well connected spy used to spend Christmas at Victor Rothschild's house, along with Dick White of MI5. In 1950, Moura Budberg reported to MI5 that Blunt was a communist, but there was no follow up to this.

In 1951, his inactivity ceased. When Philby sent Burgess back to warn Maclean, Blunt met him on his arrival at Southampton.

When Burgess left with Maclean, Blunt swept his flat to try to ensure that no incriminating material was left behind.

MI5 were aware of the close friendship between Burgess and Blunt. Blunt was subjected to a series of interrogations, in the course of which he admitted nothing. The MI5 interrogator, Skardon, gave up, claiming that there was a special carapace of secrecy around close homosexual friends like Burgess and Blunt, with Skardon also believing, surprisingly, that Blunt had revealed as much as he could to the authorities.

The breakthrough in the investigation into Blunt did not come until 1963, when the American, Michael Straight, reported that Blunt had recruited him as a Soviet agent while they were both at Cambridge. Arthur Martin of MI5 saw Blunt at the Courtauld Institute to offer him an 'absolute guarantee of no prosecution if he now told the truth'. He added that John Cairncross had already confessed, so Blunt followed suit. As well as immunity from prosecution, it was agreed to keep his spying secret for fifteen years. Queen Elizabeth had to be informed that the greatly admired art historian and Surveyor of the Queen's Pictures was a Soviet spy.

But MI5 at the time did not yet realise that they had identified the fourth and fifth members of the Soviet 'Ring of Five' and went on searching for them. Even in 1977, James Callaghan was told that they still were not sure who the 'fifth' man was! Peter Wright's subsequent attempts to push him into revealing other, non-existent spies caused Blunt to be 'no longer able to get through the day without a bottle of gin'.

In 1979, Andrew Boyle published a novel, *Climate of Treason*, in which a character clearly based on Blunt was named after the homosexual main character in E. M. Forster's novel *Maurice*. Blunt asked to see the typescript in advance of publication. The publisher refused and Blunt's request was reported in *Private Eye*.

By this time, the fifteen years were up and the new Prime Minister, Margaret Thatcher, strongly disliked the comfortable establishment practice of offering spies who had betrayed Britain's secrets to the Soviets immunity from prosecution in return for their confessions. So, to Sir Anthony Blunt's dismay, she identified the Surveyor of the Queen's pictures as a Soviet spy and stripped him of his knighthood. Blunt claimed that he had been 'led to believe' that this would never happen.

Blunt tried to explain his betrayal by quoting E. M. Forster's dictum that 'if asked to choose between betraying his friend and betraying his country, he hoped he would have the guts to betray his country'. This was a travesty, as Blunt's role in helping Burgess and Maclean to defect was not the beginning but the culmination of over twenty years as a Soviet spy, while recruiting others to do the same. The writer Julian Barnes pointed out that 'Blunt exploited, deceived, and lied to far more friends than he was loyal to … If you betray your country, you betray your friends in that country.'

Blunt broke down in tears in confessing his treason on BBC television, aged seventy-two. In his unpublished memoir, he wrote that, in Cambridge, the enthusiasm for anti-fascist activity was so great 'that I made the biggest mistake of my life'. When he was urged by Yuri Modin to defect with Burgess and Maclean, he flabbergasted Modin by saying that 'I know how your people live' and he would not be able to stand it, leading the KGB to conclude that he was 'an ideological piece of shit'. He decided that 'I would take any risk [in Britain], rather than go to Moscow'.

So, until Thatcher's announcement, he got away with it. For what he regretted was not his spying but the public exposure, resulting in ostracism and destroying his social position. Christopher Andrew, author of *Defence of the Realm*, concluded that his apology was shallow, displaying an unwillingness to acknowledge the evil he had served in spying for Stalin.

Also in 1964, in return for a promise of immunity from prosecution, John Cairncross confessed in secret to Guy Martin of MI5 to having been a Soviet spy. He too had been educated at Trinity College, Cambridge, was a pupil of Anthony Blunt and met Donald Maclean. A down to earth young Scottish Marxist with no social pretensions, he passed first in the Civil Service exam for both the domestic civil service and the Foreign Office. In 1937, by then in the Foreign Office, he was recruited as a Soviet agent by Blunt and Arnold Deutsch. Definitely heterosexual, he later published a history of polygamy admired by Graham Greene!

Code named 'Molière', his Soviet controllers urged him to apply for a post in the Government Code and Cypher School at Bletchley Park. He served there in 1942–43, working on the Ultra cyphers, before moving to MI6, where he served under Philby, without knowing that Philby too was a Soviet spy.

While at Bletchley, he smuggled out material confirming that the British were breaking the German cyphers. During the crucial battle of Kursk with the Germans, Cairncross passed to the Soviets important intelligence about German military movements. Less detailed information had been given by Churchill to Stalin.

To prevent leakage of the extent to which they had succeeded in breaking the German codes, the British were not prepared to divulge all the relevant Ultra material, with Cairncross for a time filling the gap. The Soviet archives, when opened, showed that between 1941 and 1945, Cairncross passed nearly six thousand documents to the Soviets. He also told them about British plans to develop nuclear weapons, without being in a position to provide any details.

In 1951–52, Cairncross had been questioned about his relationship with Burgess and Maclean. Notes by him on confidential White-hall discussions were found in Burgess's flat. He admitted having in the past been a member of the Communist Party but nothing more. There were insufficient grounds to prosecute him, but he was suspended and then resigned from the position he held at that time in the Treasury.

It was not until 1964 that Cairncross, by then teaching in the United States, admitted to Arthur Martin of MI5 that he had spied for the Soviets. Like Blunt, Cairncross did not want to end up in Moscow. He stayed overseas until, in 1970, he was offered some immunity from prosecution.

MI5 did not yet realise how highly Cairncross had been rated as a spy by the Soviets; more so than Blunt. It was not until 1979 that his spying became public knowledge, when he gave an interview to the journalist, Barrie Penrose. Oleg Gordievsky subsequently confirmed that Cairncross was indeed the fifth member of the 'Ring of Five'.

Some in the press were very disappointed that the 'fifth' man had turned out to be someone as apparently boring as John Cairncross. There continued to be speculation about Victor Rothschild.

At Trinity College, Cambridge, he had befriended Burgess, Blunt and Philby. His flat in London was shared with Burgess and Blunt. He had served with distinction in MI5 during the war, including demonstrating his skill in disarming explosives. Yuri Modin at one stage identified him as a member of the Cambridge spy ring then recanted. Rothschild later became head of the Central Policy Review Staff, the so called 'think tank', under Margaret Thatcher. There was no evidence that he had ever been a Soviet spy.

But in a further effort to clear his name in the popular press, Rothschild took the extraordinary step of collaborating with and part financing Peter Wright's book, written with David Greengrass, *Spycatcher*. As Rothschild's biographer observed, 'So little guilt did Victor feel at procuring that colossal breach of security that he continued to address letters to the *Times* deploring the steady leak of classified documents to the press'. Rothschild clearly had the skills in deception that would have made him a successful secret agent. But as Soviet sources later confirmed, he wasn't one.

As it was advertised as an account of how Wright and his colleagues had 'burgled and bugged their way' all over London, the government did everything it could to stop the publication of *Spycatcher*. It succeeded for a time in Britain. The Cabinet Secretary, Sir Robert Armstrong, was sent on a suicide mission to try to stop its publication in Australia. In court there, he was confronted by a jeering press gallery and an aggressive young lawyer, Malcolm Turnbull, who used the case to jet propel his political career; it helped him eventually to become the Australian Prime Minister. At one point, accused of lying, Armstrong brought the house down by suggesting instead that he was 'being economical with the truth!' The book was published in Australia and eventually in Britain in 1988.

The activities of the Cambridge spies and the fools they made of the British authorities generated a huge new chapter in the media coverage of espionage. Philby contended, justifiably, that their success in doing so was due to the British class system at the time. He had not been found out because he was regarded as 'one of us'. Much the same applied to Burgess, Maclean and Anthony Blunt.

Far from hiding, Burgess, Maclean and Philby all had advertised their far left sentiments at Cambridge. As instructed by Deutsch, they then covered their tracks. No attempt was made to check if they had actually joined the Communist Party, as both Burgess and Maclean had done.

Of the three principal Cambridge spies, Burgess found it hardest to adapt to life in Soviet Russia, starting in the industrial city of Kuybyshev, which he described as 'permanently like Glasgow on a Saturday night'. He had not been identified as a Soviet agent up to the time of his defection and initially dreamed of returning to Britain. In 1954, Vladmir Petrov, a senior KGB officer who defected in Australia, confirmed Burgess's spying activities and that he and Maclean were living in Moscow.

As Burgess still toyed with the idea of returning, the Foreign Office declared that he would be arrested if he did (even though they still were uncertain of securing a conviction). He met a string of British visitors, including Tom Driberg, who, with similar tastes and politics, wrote a would be sympathetic book about him. The actress Coral Browne and the actor and director Michael Redgrave also met him there. But they found the former socialite living a very lonely existence.

Alan Bennett's play *An Englishman Abroad* was about Burgess in exile. In his further play *Single Spies*, Bennett contended that 'no one has ever shown that Burgess did much harm, except to make fools of people in high places'. This was a minority view. Burgess was not as valuable to the Soviets as Philby or Maclean, simply doing as much damage as he could, in the course of which he did indeed make fools of people in high places. Burgess also featured in Julian Mitchell's 1981 play *Another Country*, in its 1984 film adaptation and in several novels and numerous television productions.

Burgess was introduced by the Russians to a male companion to whom he became attached, but drank himself to death at the age of fifty-two. Philby never forgave him for ignoring his instruction not to abscond with Maclean and refused to have anything to do with him in Moscow, even when Burgess was dying.

In contrast to Burgess, Maclean made the most of his new life in Moscow, learning Russian, earning a doctorate and serving as an expert on Britain, Western economic policy and NATO. He worked directly in the Soviet Foreign Ministry and for the institutes and publications it controlled.

Melinda Maclean, with their children, had followed him to Moscow, but following Philby's arrival there, she had a three year affair with him. In 1979, she returned to the United States, where she never disclosed any of her own secret activities. Two of their children married in Russia but ended up living in Britain or the US.

While remaining staunchly communist and entirely unrepentant, Maclean did not find Russia a socialist utopia. Shortly before his death, he wrote a critique of what he regarded as the retrograde development of Soviet society. His book on *British Foreign Policy since Suez*, criticising the UK's alignment with the United States, was published a year after he died.

Philby did not arrive in Moscow until 1963. In 1967, he gave an interview in Moscow to Murray Sayle of *The Times*, confirming that he had worked for the KGB and declaring that 'his purpose in life was to destroy imperialism'. In the following year, *My Silent War* was published in Britain.

Modin said of Philby that 'he never revealed his true self. Neither the British, nor the women he lived with, nor ourselves [the KGB] ever managed to pierce the armour of mystery that clad him.' Modin's book *My Five Cambridge Friends* was published in 1994.

A year after arriving in Moscow, Philby embarked on his aforementioned affair with Melinda Maclean, putting an end to his friendship with her husband. Though claiming nostalgia for Worcester sauce, Colman's mustard and Lyons' tea houses and, every day, reading *The Times* and listening to the BBC World Service, he adapted to life in Moscow by working for the KGB propaganda team, inserting 'sinister' fake passages in published US and CIA documents.

In 1971, having been introduced to her by his fellow Soviet spy, George Blake, he married a much younger Russian/Polish woman, Rufina Pukhova, who wrote an affectionate book about him: *The Private Life of Kim Philby: The Moscow Years*. Rufina later described him as 'disappointed in many ways' by what he found in Moscow. 'He saw people suffering too much,' while arguing that 'the ideals were right, but the way they were carried out was wrong. The fault lay with the people in charge.' He asked, 'Why do old people live so badly here? After all, they won the war.' She reported that, in his early years in Moscow, he had attempted to commit suicide by cutting his wrists. Their marriage was difficult because of his drinking, which he cut back to save it, and bouts of depression. He died, covered with Soviet honours, in 1988.

CHAPTER XIII

BLAKE AND HIS ESCAPE

The next really important British traitor, George Blake, was not another well connected member of the British upper crust but pretty much the opposite. There was no connection with the original Cambridge spies. He only met Philby and Maclean when he got to Moscow.

Born George Behar, his mother was Dutch; his father, who served with the British Army in the First World War, was Egyptian Jewish. His name later was changed to Blake. While being educated at the English school in Cairo, he became close to his cousin, Henri Curiel, who later became head of the Communist Party in Egypt. During the war, he was interned briefly as a youthful member of the Dutch resistance.

On escaping to Britain, he joined the Royal Navy as a sub-lieutenant then was recruited by MI6 in 1944. The Navy sent him to Cambridge to study languages, including Russian. In 1948, he was posted to the British mission in South Korea, becoming a prisoner of war from 1950, when Seoul was captured by the North Koreans. In the course of his three year detention, it was, he said, studying Karl Marx that persuaded him to become a communist and volunteer to work for the KGB.

On his release and return to Britain in 1954, he married an MI6 secretary, Gillian Allan. He was posted by MI6 to Berlin, where he informed his KGB contacts of British and American agents and operations, including the tunnel they had constructed to monitor Soviet communications. The Russians were so concerned to protect Blake as their source that they continued to use the monitored communications for a further year.

Blake later acknowledged having betrayed to the Soviets all the British agents in East Germany and Eastern Europe that he knew about, saying, 'I don't know what I handed over because it was so much.' He also probably exposed a CIA agent in Russian military intelligence, P. S. Popov, who was executed in 1960. In the following year, he was denounced by a Polish defector. Under interrogation, Blake said that he had not been tortured in North Korea – he had changed sides voluntarily, making a full confession.

Under Article I of the Official Secrets Act, the maximum sentence for each offence was fourteen years. But in May 1961, Blake was sentenced by the Lord Chief Justice at an *in camera* trial to fourteen years in prison on three separate charges, the sentences to be served consecutively, not concurrently, so forty-two years.

The severity of this sentence was due to the conviction that, unlike Burgess and Maclean, who did not have blood on their hands, but like Philby, he had been responsible for the executions of numerous MI6 contacts, as was confirmed subsequently by General Oleg Kalugin of the KGB, who said that Blake had asked for assurances that the people he denounced would not be killed, but of course, most of them were. Blake acknowledged this himself, 'apologising' in 1991 for the people he had caused to be killed.

Five years into his sentence, Blake was enabled to escape from Wormwood Scrubs by three former prisoners – an Irish republican and two anti-nuclear activists, with financial support from the film director, Tony Richardson. He was smuggled in a camper van back to his comrades in East Germany.

He moved on to Moscow, where he introduced Philby to his future wife. As he survived until ninety-eight, he lived to see the end of communism and of the Soviet Union. His death in 2020 was marked by a warm tribute from his former KGB colleague Vladimir Putin, describing him as 'a brilliant professional'.

Although he had done as much damage as any of them, because he had not been 'one of us', a member of the British elite, Blake did not receive anything like the same amount of media and literary attention as the Cambridge spies. He argued that he did not betray his country, because he had never really belonged to it. Simon Gray wrote a play, *Cell Mates*, about Blake and his Irish rescuer, Sean Bourke. Alfred Hitchcock planned to make a film about his escape but died before being able to do so. In 2015, the BBC made a television documentary, including interviewing him. In 2021, they broadcast a radio play about his escape. Blake also appears as a character in Ian McEwan's novel *The Innocent*.

CHAPTER XIV

THE MOST IMPORTANT
OF ALL SPIES?

Klaus Fuchs, a physicist and communist refugee from Germany, initially was interned on his arrival in Britain, but from 1941 he was assigned to research on the atomic weapons 'Tube Alloys' programme because he was rated so highly as a nuclear physicist by one of its leaders, Rudolf Peierls. The overriding concern was to produce a nuclear device before anyone else did and Peierls did not want to have to try to do so without him. Fuchs began passing information on the programme to a KGB major code named 'Sonya'. From 1943, he worked on the Manhattan Project to develop nuclear weapons at the Los Alamos laboratory in the US. His special expertise was on the phenomenon of implosion necessary for the development of the plutonium bomb.

Meanwhile, US cryptologists were engaged in a sustained effort · to intercept messages to and from the main Soviet intelligence agencies. Codes based on the One Time Pad process were unbreakable unless an operator made a mistake or duplicate pages were used. So, most of this traffic could not be intercepted, but some of it, often in fragmentary form, was.

The intercepts revealed espionage by Julius and Ethel Rosenberg and Klaus Fuchs. In April 1945, Fuchs was congratulated by Moscow on having provided information 'of great value', including data on 'the atomic mass of the nuclear explosive' and 'the explosive method of actuating' the atomic bomb. According to Russian sources, Fuchs provided the Soviets with the first information on the electromagnetic separation of uranium and the primary explosion needed to start the chain reaction, as well as a detailed technical report, with the specifications for both fission bombs. On being arrested, in January 1950, to the horror of Philby, Fuchs confessed to having passed information to the Soviets since 1942.

He told Peierls that he had done so because he believed that knowledge of atomic research should not be the property of any one country but should be shared for the benefit of mankind. In reality, he feared that it could give the United States a decisive advantage vis-à-vis the Soviet Union. He was sentenced to fourteen years' imprisonment. Released after nine years, he left for East Germany.

Fourteen years was the maximum penalty in Britain for breaching the Official Secrets Act. Whitehall lawyers advised that Fuchs should not be charged with espionage, as Soviet Russia had been an ally. This despite the fact that they had not been allies for the past five years, which they had devoted to subjugating Eastern Europe, while Fuchs continued his espionage.

Apart from the United States' nuclear plans, the Rosenbergs had provided the Russians with top secret information about US sonar, radar and jet propulsion systems. Despite an international outcry, the Rosenbergs were executed – the only time the death penalty has been invoked in the US for espionage. The sentence was especially harsh for Ethel Rosenberg, who had been an active collaborator but not the principal. After their execution, a huge campaign was mounted to suggest that they had been innocent, only for Russian sources then to confirm that they had been highly valued Soviet agents.

Described in Frank Close's 2019 book *Trinity* as 'the most important spy in history', Fuchs was the most valuable to the Soviets of the atom spies. They had the theoretical knowledge to develop a nuclear weapon but were lagging way behind the Americans in its practical application. The Soviet Union tested its own first nuclear weapon in August 1949 – sooner than the Americans had expected. It was around this time that Fuchs left Los Alamos, presumably feeling that he had by then done as much for the Soviets as he could. He already had transferred to them his knowledge of the designs for the plutonium bomb and the fusion hydrogen bomb so that, within a year of the first US hydrogen bomb test in 1952, the Soviet Union was able to successfully test its hydrogen bomb. The consensus among both Western and Soviet nuclear scientists has been that the Soviet Union would have been able to develop nuclear weapons anyway but that Fuchs accelerated the process for them. Philby and the other Cambridge spies combined could not begin to rival Fuchs for the value of the secret information he provided, though they attracted a vast amount more media attention.

So how did it come about that J. Robert Oppenheimer, overall director of the Manhattan Project that produced the first atomic weapons, subsequently had his US security clearance withdrawn?

Oppenheimer was a character straight out of a novel by Graham Greene, whose tortured and sometimes tortuous nature was powerfully portrayed in Christopher Nolan's 2024 film, which was mainly accurate, though inventing the exchanges with Einstein. The most brilliant of nuclear physicists, he regarded himself also as a philosopher. Too arrogant to be likeable, he was unscrupulous in his personal life. As his rival and nemesis Edward Teller observed, he experienced little difficulty in holding contradictory opinions at the same time. Never formally a member of the Communist Party, he described himself later as having been a fellow traveller. Nearly all his friends were communists, as was his girlfriend, Jean Tatlock (who tragically killed herself), his brother and his wife. When he joined the Manhattan Project in 1942, he wrote on his security questionnaire the 'half-jocular' statement that he had been 'a member of just about every communist front organisation on the West Coast'.

As a result of these associations, he was under intense suspicion from the FBI. Yet he was regarded as so crucial to success that the Pentagon officer in charge of the programme, General Leslie Groves, insisted that Oppenheimer must run it. Groves ordered that Oppenheimer must receive a security clearance 'without delay, irrespective of any' of the damaging information he knew to be held about him. For he detected in Oppenheimer great technical expertise, plus an 'overweening ambition'.

In July 1945, Oppenheimer was present at the first test of the atomic bomb in the New Mexico desert. Having witnessed the blinding flash, realising that 'the world had changed' he later quoted the *Bhagavad Gita*, 'Now I am become Death, the destroyer of worlds.' But at the time, it was a huge relief to him that, as he said on witnessing the test explosion, 'I guess it worked.'

He also was in an excited mood on the eve of the nuclear bombing of Hiroshima, saying that it was a pity that the weapon had not been developed in time to be used on Nazi Germany. Subsequently, he deplored the follow on bombing of Nagasaki. In a meeting with Truman in October 1945, he said that he felt he had 'blood on his hands', infuriating the President, who had had to take the decision to *use* nuclear weapons. Truman had no regrets about doing so, as the only way to end the war with Japan without staging an invasion that would have cost an incalculable number of US and Allied lives.

Oppenheimer then argued that atomic weapons should be brought under international control and that US knowledge should be shared with others, including, in effect, the Soviets. This debate did result in Bernard Baruch's plan to bring civil nuclear production under international control through the creation of the International Atomic Energy Authority. What cost Oppenheimer his security clearance was his opposition to the development by the US of the even more powerful hydrogen bomb, to the annoyance of its main architect Edward Teller, only for it to transpire that, with the help of Klaus Fuchs, the Soviet Union was far advanced with a similar programme.

In some bizarre testimony, Oppenheimer admitted having denounced his colleague George Eltenton as a potential Soviet agent to protect his communist friend Haakon Chevalier, who had told him that he had means of passing information to the Soviet Union. Yet Oppenheimer had removed a number of people who had Soviet sympathies from the programme.

Soviet sources confirmed subsequently that Oppenheimer had never spied for the Soviet Union, though they had regarded him as a covert member of the Communist Party in the 1930s. Over five decades after his death, in 2022 the withdrawal of his security clearance was solemnly revoked by the Biden administration.

The fear of Fuchs and, to some extent, Oppenheimer that the US might abuse its short lived monopoly of nuclear weapons proved to be unfounded. When General MacArthur flirted with using nuclear weapons against China in the Korean War, Truman vetoed any idea of doing so. If Stalin had got there first, he would have been unlikely to act with similar restraint.

Elizabeth I's spymaster, Sir Francis Walsingham.

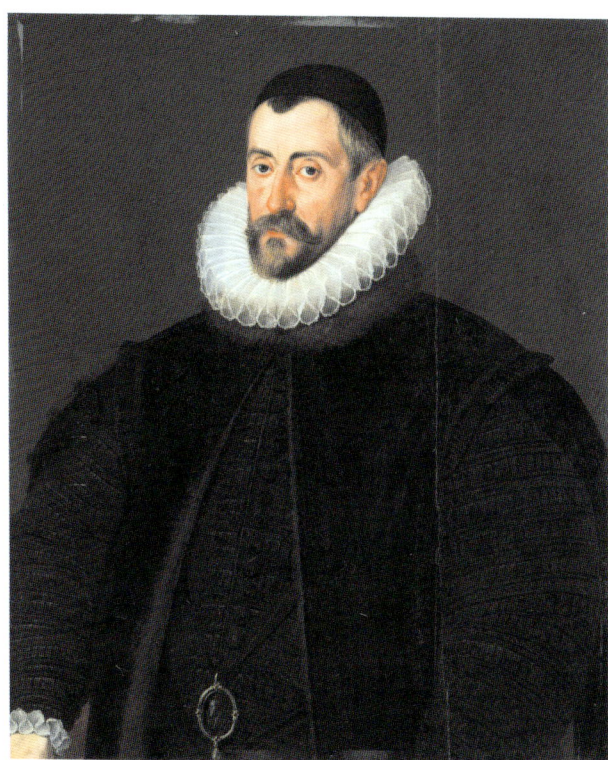

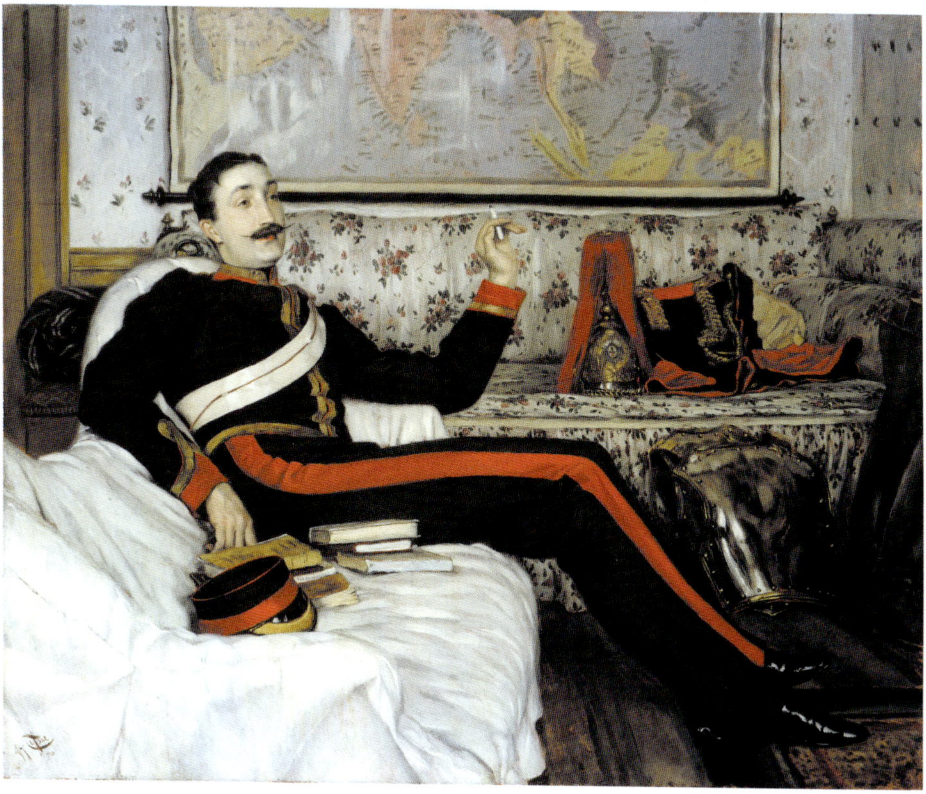

Colonel Fred Burnaby, 1870.

Sidney Reilly, the so called 'ace of spies'. © Hulton Archive / Stringer / Getty Images

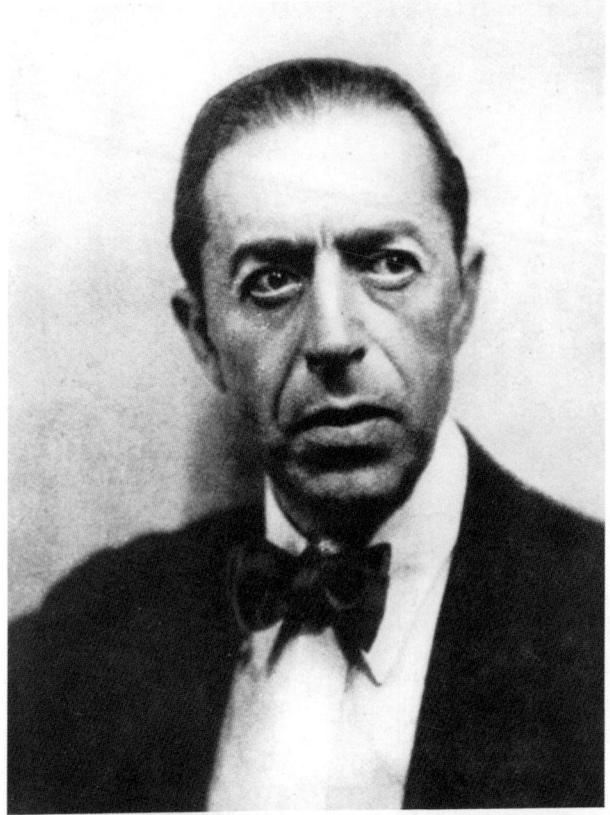

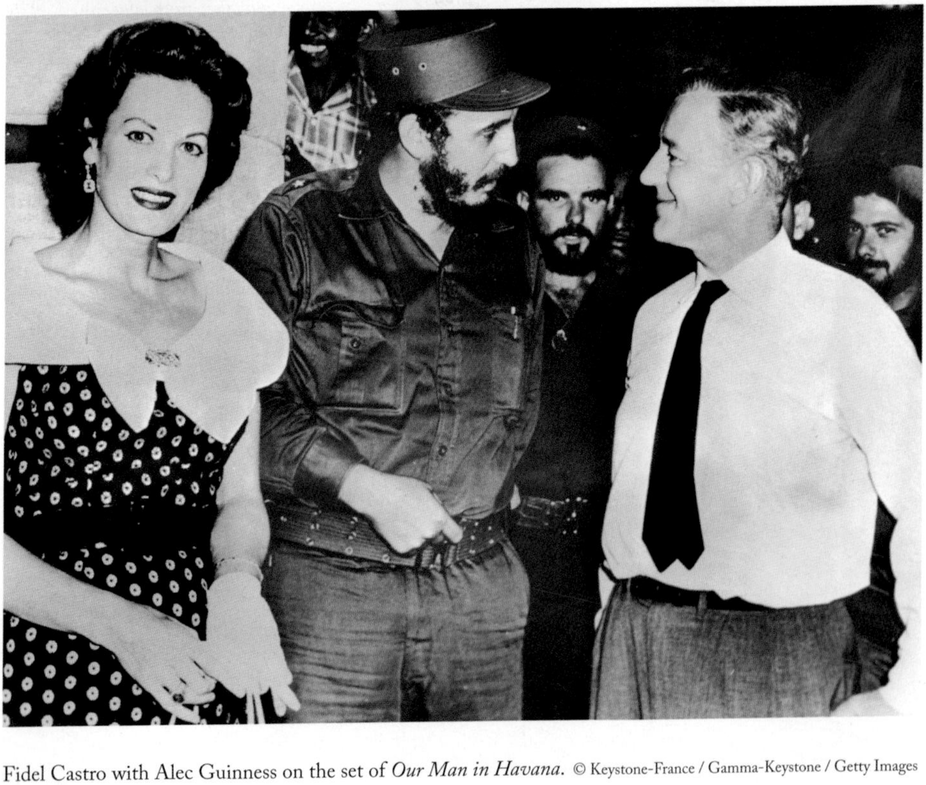

Fidel Castro with Alec Guinness on the set of *Our Man in Havana*. © Keystone-France / Gamma-Keystone / Getty Images

ABOVE Harold 'Kim' Philby, celebrating being 'cleared' by Harold Macmillan, 1955.

© Keystone / Hulton Archive / Getty Images

LEFT Ian Fleming in Room 39, naval intelligence.

© Spaarnestad Photo / Bridgeman Images

Sean Connery and Ian Fleming on the set of *Dr. No.* © Sunset Boulevard / Corbis / Getty Images

Ian Fleming and Ursula Andress on the set of *Dr. No.* © Bettmann / Getty Images

Sean Connery and Ursula Andress; handstands on the set of *Dr. No*.
© Hulton Archive / Stringer / Getty Images, United Artist / Archive Photos / Stringer / Getty Images

Barbara Bach on the set
of *The Spy Who Loved Me*.
© Sunset Boulevard / Corbis / Getty Images

Eva Green, *femme fatale* in *Casino Royale*.
© Imago / ZUMA Press Wire

Alec Guinness excelling as George Smiley. © BBC Photo Archive

Alan Turing.
© National Portrait Gallery

Colossus machine, Bletchley Park. © Steve Simmons / Alamy Stock Photo

Wrens operating the Colossus machine. © SSLP / Bletchley Park Trust / Getty Images

Oleg Gordievsky with President Ronald Reagan, 1987. © Eraza Collection / Alamy Stock photo

CHAPTER XV

FROM ENIGMA
TO COLOSSUS

Dillwyn ('Dilly') Knox and Nigel de Grey had worked on the decoding of the Zimmermann telegram in the First World War. It was the French *Deuxième Bureau* who alerted the British to the work of the Polish cryptographers, led by Marian Rejewski, seeking to break encryption on the German Enigma machines. At a conference with the Poles in July 1939, Rejewski was extremely impressed by Knox's technical competence. Two reconstructed German Enigma machines were handed over to the British and French. Thereafter, Knox's 'rodding' system, then Alan Turing's decoding machines (bombes) enabled the British to decipher the Abwehr traffic and the Italian naval codes. After the battle of Matapan, in which he sank much of the Italian Navy, Admiral Cunningham went to their headquarters at Bletchley Park to congratulate Knox and 'your girls'. Knox died in 1943 but, by the end of the war, Bletchley Park had decrypted 140,000 Abwehr messages.

When the Germans started using the different Lorenz cypher system, it too was attacked, with only partial but critical success, as it carried the German strategic military traffic. The results were so important that extracts from the resultant material, codenamed Ultra, had to be channelled to the Allied commanders in the field without most of them knowing where it came from. Sir Stewart Menzies, head of MI6, had no direct involvement with Bletchley, other than supporting funding for them. But the fact that he was the channel for Ultra material to be seen by Churchill enormously enhanced his reputation. The resultant foreknowledge of German military plans and movements was credited by Eisenhower with having materially shortened the war.

When the United States entered the war, in a late night *tête-à-tête* in the White House, Churchill confessed to Roosevelt that the British had broken the US diplomatic codes, which he had stopped now that they were allies. By the end of the war, many thousands of people were employed at Bletchley Park, yet for the next thirty years there were no leaks from any of them. But in 1973, a French writer, Gustave Bertrand, revealed a great deal in his book *L'Enigme*. This effectively enabled Frederick Winterbotham to publish, in the following year, *The Ultra Secret* without being prosecuted. Winterbotham had no involvement in the actual code breaking. His role had been to help to distribute extracts from the product to commanders in the field.

His book, written from memory, contained numerous errors, the most spectacular of which was his assertion that, to protect Ultra, Churchill allowed Coventry to be bombed with no interference from the RAF. The wartime records showed that this was nonsense. Churchill thought that the raid was planned against London.

The publication did a great deal for the mystique of the British code breakers and their contribution to winning the war but was disliked by the cryptographers themselves, who considered that it revealed too much about their extraordinary capabilities. This was an area of expertise in which the British at the time were ahead of their closest allies. American commanders from Eisenhower down came to rely on the intelligence they received from Ultra. The Anglo-American sharing of intelligence during the war, including signals intelligence, has continued to this day, with the 'five eyes' system subsequently extending the sharing of some signals intelligence with Australia, Canada and New Zealand as well.

While the public were and still are fascinated by the Ultra story, it did not prove easy to write a novel or a play about brilliant people attempting to solve complex mathematical and linguistic problems behind their computers in Nissen huts. But in 2001, Mick Jagger helped to finance a fictionalised film version: *Enigma*, starring Kate Winslet and Saffron Burrows.

One of the absolutely key figures at Bletchley, inventor of the Turing machine and author of the 'Turing proof', Alan Turing was the most brilliant mathematician and computer designer of all. He led the team at Hut 8, the section responsible for naval cryptanalysis. Turing invented the bombes crucial for speeding up cryptanalysis by seeking to replicate the Enigma settings.

By 1944, a Bletchley Park team led by the mathematician Maxwell Newman and the engineer Thomas Flowers, inspired by Turing, had developed a set of computers called Colossus to attack the Lorenz cypher, making it *the first programmable, electronic, digital computer*, with Britain thereby leading the world in the computerisation of espionage. Colossus reduced the time it took to decipher Lorenz messages from what could be weeks to hours – of vital importance in the Normandy landings and the campaign in France.

The machines were operated mainly by Wrens (Women's Royal Naval Service). Around 7,500 young women ended up working at Bletchley, where it was a code of honour not to tell even their families what they were doing there. During his visit to Bletchley Park in 1941, Churchill described it as 'the goose that laid the golden eggs but never cackled'.

Alan Turing had a non sexual romance with and proposed to a fellow worker there, Joan Clarke, but then admitted that he was homosexual, so he felt unable to go ahead with the marriage. He left Bletchley to take up research posts at the end of the war, receiving the Order of the British Empire (OBE) for his service there.

Seven years later, Turing was prosecuted for homosexual acts. However strange this may seem today, homosexuality between consenting adults was not legalised in Britain until 1967. Turing accepted a hormone treatment regarded as amounting to chemical castration as an alternative to prison. Two years later, he died at forty-one in an apparent suicide from cyanide poisoning.

In response to a public campaign, in 2009 the British Prime Minister, Gordon Brown, made an official apology for the 'appalling way' Turing was treated. Queen Elizabeth granted a posthumous pardon. The 2017 'Alan Turing law' pardoned men convicted under the historical ban on homosexuality. In 2019, a BBC series was devoted to him and his portrait appears on the current Bank of England £50 note.

His legacy has been honoured at Cambridge, Stanford, Princeton and other universities worldwide in cases too numerous to list.

The bust of Turing by Eduardo Paolozzi is displayed at Edinburgh University. In 1996, Turing was played by Derek Jacobi in the play *Breaking the Code*, a notable fictional version of his life and work. In the 2014 film *The Imitation Game*, Turing was played by Benedict Cumberbatch, with Keira Knightley as Joan Clarke. The film got an excellent critical reception and was the most popular and successful independent film in that year, attracting for the team of code breakers at Bletchley Park as well as Turing the acclaim they deserved.

Alan Turing was ushering us all into a new world, including in intelligence. While the First World War had demonstrated the vital importance of SIGINT (signals intelligence) under Admiral Hall, Bletchley Park and the Second World War demonstrated just how and why SIGINT had a credibility far higher than most HUMINT (human intelligence). Colonel Penkovsky and Oleg Gordievsky and, for the Soviets, Klaus Fuchs and the Cambridge spies demonstrated the major contribution human intelligence could still make, but greater credibility henceforth was given to what the country's enemies were saying to each other, unaware that their supposedly unbreakable codes had in fact been broken.

CHAPTER XVI

IAN FLEMING

In 1962, David Bruce, the very sophisticated US Ambassador to Britain, a wartime colleague from his days in the Office for Strategic Services (OSS), reported, 'I bought six of Ian Fleming's adventure stories. They bid fair to ruin my health; for three nights running, I have read until three in the morning.'

There is a reason why Ian Fleming became the world's most successful spy writer, and it was not just the films made from his novels. Anyone who doubts his 'mesmeric readability' or believes, like Paul Johnson, that 'Mr Fleming cannot write', should try reading or re-reading a few of the books he actually wrote, starting, for instance, with *From Russia, with Love* or *Diamonds are Forever*. If they do, they may suffer the same fate as David Bruce. Ian Fleming wrote his tales of espionage for an audience that, apparently, could never get enough of them.

He believed that, to write a good thriller, you needed to have an exciting life. The descriptive parts of every novel were based to a large extent on his own experiences. If you want to find a model for

James Bond, look no further than the author, whose tastes in drinks, cigarettes, way of life and women are mirrored by his subject.

Ian Fleming had served in the world of intelligence long enough to know it very well. What was lacking in his experience and had to be invented were, precisely, the scenes of action that, as a staff officer, for the most part, he had *not* participated in during the war. For those, he needed to rely on his imagination.

He was helped by never taking his storylines too seriously. His purpose, he insisted, was *entertainment* and no higher than that. When his admirer, Raymond Chandler, urged him to aim higher by making his stories more realistic (more like Chandler's), his reply was that Bond lay somewhere between a fantasy and the 'blunt instrument of a government department'. Bond was intended to be 'what every man would like to be and what every woman would like to have between her sheets' – in their dreams.

So, they were easy to make fun of, as his wife's more refined, though less successful, literary friends and many others enjoyed doing. But it was his imagined hero, helped by the spectacular cinematography of the films, that sold over a hundred million books and filled the cinemas worldwide. So much so that even the films most disparaged by the critics, *in every case*, were a spectacular commercial success. *The Man with the Golden Gun* was rated a 'flop' because it had one of the lowest takings of any Bond movie, at 'only' $97.6 million. No wonder, therefore, that Cubby Broccoli and co. were so anxious to keep the franchise alive, thanks to spectacular cinematography and excellent screenwriters, when Ian Fleming died.

His writing style, he claimed, was forged in the hard school of editing Reuters news reports, which needed to be accurate, succinct, direct and to capture the readers' attention straight away. What he aimed for in his writing was to generate and maintain a fast pace, with no impediments to doing so. A serious bibliophile and vastly well read, he was an ardent admirer of Hemingway. While never pretending to aim anything like as high, he did seek to emulate what he regarded as a masculine, stripped down style, with the avoidance of bells and whistles and any literary flourishes.

Anthony Burgess noted his use of convincing detail to anchor his reader to some form of reality, followed by a 'speed of narrative, which hustles the reader past each danger point of mockery'. Umberto Eco, author of *The Name of the Rose*, wrote an entire essay about Ian Fleming's style, which he described as having 'a rhythm, a polish, a certain sensuous feeling for words', concluding that 'Fleming is more literate than he gives one to understand'.

Described, even by his critics, as knowing 'all the tricks of the trade', what came to him instinctively, the most important art of the storyteller, was to encourage and, if possible, *oblige* the reader to turn the page or start the next chapter, to find out what happened next. The story and the writing, therefore, needed to be fast paced, with a sufficient number of twists and turns.

So, how exciting was Ian Fleming's life and how did it lead him towards this spectacular result?

Born in Mayfair in 1908, he was the grandson of Robert Fleming. An impoverished young Scot working for a jute company in Dundee, having been sent on an assignment in America, Robert Fleming returned convinced that fortunes could be made by investing there, but it was too difficult for individual investors to access the opportunity.

So, he founded the Scottish American Investment Trust, one of the two very first investment trusts and precursor of all the future unit trusts, enabling those wishing to invest in the US to pool their savings to do so. He then concentrated their investments mainly on financing the badly needed development of the new railroad network in the United States, with very impressive results. He founded the Robert Fleming & Co. investment bank, having created a hugely profitable investment management business.

So, Ian Fleming and his elder brother Peter were born, apparently, with many advantages. But in 1917, when Ian was nine years old, their father, Valentine, was killed by German artillery fire on the Western Front. Valentine had been the MP for Henley. Winston Churchill wrote his obituary. In later life, Ian always displayed a copy of it, signed by Churchill, in his various homes.

Several years after their father's death, their formidable mother, Evelyn (Eve), had an affair with the artist Augustus John, who painted portraits of her. This resulted in the birth in 1925 of their half-sister, Amaryllis Fleming, who became a well known cellist. Eve disappeared on a long journey overseas. On her return, she announced that she had adopted the child. It was said of Augustus John that as he walked down the King's Road, he always patted the heads of any children he met, in case they were his own.

In her bohemian phase, Eve bought three cottages at the end of the King's Road, rebuilt them together and christened them Turner House after the painter's studio there where, loving the Thames, he painted towards the end of his life.

Fleming was taught by his mother that his father had been perfect and, unfortunately for him, the same soon started to be said about his more cerebral elder brother, Peter, who was far better behaved. As children, the two fought a lot but ended up with a strong affection for each other.

Peter and Ian both went to Eton, where Peter excelled as a scholar, while Ian became the *victor ludorum* (winner of the games) two years running. Ian claimed later that his victory in a steeplechase had been helped by a prior caning. The torture by caning scene in *Casino Royale* must presumably have owed something to his experiences at Eton. While there, he edited quite a successful small newspaper for the boys and their parents, called *The Wyvern*. With his mother's help, it included sketches by Augustus John.

While Peter was destined for Oxford, where he won first class honours, Ian was thought more suitable for a career in the Army. The head of the army crammer he attended to prepare for Sandhurst told his mother that he ought to make an excellent soldier, provided he was not ruined by 'the ladies'. In his first term, he was a middling student at Sandhurst but could not stand the constant parading and not being allowed out at night. He fell for a pretty blonde called Peggy Barnard. But then, in a Soho club, he managed to contract gonorrhoea.

His furious mother told him that he had let down the entire family. He applied for leave from Sandhurst but then resigned. In the hope of improving his languages and behaviour, he was sent to the Villa Tennerhof in Kitzbühel for further education. This was run by Ernan Forbes Dennis, formerly of the British Army and MI6, and his wife, the author Phyllis Bottome. Ian was made to read the German classics and to do some writing.

Both Peter and Ian were extremely good looking. A bevy of Austrian girls arranged for the prettiest to trip over the sprawling Ian, so that they could all get to know him. He made the most of his good fortune, while pining for the English Deirdre Hart-Davis. Hiking in the mountains, sometimes overnight, helped to provide the Alpine background for *On Her Majesty's Secret Service*.

As Ian devoted his energies to his role as a Kitzbühel Casanova, displaying an 'unstoppable desire to make conquests of women', little to his studies and had been rude to his wife, Forbes Dennis threatened him with expulsion from the Tennerhof. To save himself, in a major turning point for him, Ian wrote an abject apology, promising to take the programme more seriously, which thereafter he did.

In 1928, he attended a preliminary interview for the Foreign Service. As Ian was interested in psychoanalysis, while he was in Munich, Forbes Dennis arranged for him to meet Dr Self, a colleague of Alfred Adler, who contended that many neuroses stemmed from a feeling of inferiority vis-à-vis an elder brother. Having met Eve as she swept through on a visit, Dr Self told Forbes Dennis that, with a mother like that, he could see little hope for Ian! But Ian's reaction was to write an amusing note about her semi-regal progress through the city.

Ian, meanwhile, had developed a passion for motor cars. He was determined to lead what he described as 'a fast car life'. In his modest Standard tourer, driven at breakneck speed around Kitzbühel, he had tried to navigate a level crossing at the same time as a train. He now reported the thrill of driving a friend's Bugatti at a hundred miles an hour near Henley. By this time also, he had befriended the future publisher Rupert Hart-Davis and the poet William Plomer and had started collecting the first editions of important books.

Sent to Geneva by Forbes Dennis, he reacted to what he regarded as excessive Swiss orderliness and smugness by racing around in a flashy Buick two seater. Through contacts with International Labour Organization people in Geneva, he got a holiday job at the League of Nations in Geneva, only for him to conclude that international bureaucracies wasted a great deal of money, turned out far too much paper 'and achieved very little'.

The Tennerhof had been the making of Ian, who had become a voracious reader. In that respect, the supposedly middlebrow Ian Fleming, who could read in French and German plus a smattering of Russian, was fully the equal of most of his future wife's literary friends, who enjoyed looking down on him. His tastes were catholic, including Raymond Chandler, but also Lermontov, Adler, Mann, Kafka, Waugh, Greene and Hemingway. Lermontov's *A Hero of Our Time* was Tatiana's favourite book in *From Russia, with Love*.

By now he had fallen heavily for a local beauty called Monique Panchaud, daughter of a wealthy landowner, to whom he was engaged for three years. He returned to London to sit the written part of the Foreign Office exam. Even though he reached a pass standard, he was not offered a post, which went only to the top three in the competition.

Eve claimed that Monique had distracted him from his studies but encouraged him to write to Sir Roderick Jones, the head of Reuters, whom she had befriended. Ian did so, emphasising his international education and, following interviews, was taken on by them in October 1931. But Monique got a ghastly reception from his mother when she arrived to stay at Turner House. Eve did not want her son marrying a Swiss bourgeoise, so she threatened to cut off all financial support if Ian did not break off their engagement. The furious Panchaud family threatened to sue and he had to make a payment to them.

Having decided henceforth to adopt a utilitarian attitude towards women, he embarked on affairs with Maud Russell, a banker's wife who was seventeen years older than him, and the wild, much younger Olivia Campbell. He also enjoyed a tryst in his mother's Daimler with a 'rather spiffing' dancer called Storm. His mother was perplexed to find the rear of the Daimler full of black boa feathers.

For Reuters, he provided a colourful account of the show trial in Moscow of six employees of a British engineering company. But his grandfather had died without leaving any of his fortune to Eve and her children, and Ian was told that in future he would have to finance his own expensive tastes. So he left Reuters, with regret, as he had done well and enjoyed working there. It was at Reuters, he always said later, that he learned how to write clearly and concisely. He regarded the training in style of writing he received there as far superior to that at Eton. He had been obliged to perfect 'the art of simplification'. His copy *had* to be concise, vivid and accurate.

But he was not prepared to give up his hoped for lifestyle. Maud Russell engineered for him the chance to become a partner in a small merchant bank called Cull & Co., run by her husband. Cull & Co. soon fell on hard times and Ian Fleming proved to be of little use at banking since, as a friend observed, he simply wanted a job that would give him 'leisure and money enough for an entertaining life.' He had joined the now defunct St James's Club, before moving on to White's, then Boodles and the Portland Club to play bridge.

With his group of male friends, many evenings were devoted to bridge. At weekends, they would set off together to play golf, venturing as far afield as Deauville and Gleneagles. At the casino in Deauville, he played only for modest stakes but loved the atmosphere in which baccarat was played in the green baize gaming room, admiring the cool, professional skill of the syndicate's main dealer.

He had been due to be best man at the wedding of his friend Martin Hill but could not attend. He made up for this by having a fling with his friend's bride. As she observed, 'He thought he could get away with murder.' So, presumably, did she.

He moved from Cull & Co. to Rowe and Pitman stockbrokers, where he was a golfing friend of Hugh Smith, one of the partners. Ian stayed there for four years, only for Smith subsequently to described him as 'the world's worst stockbroker', as he was not interested in the business. He enjoyed lunching clients at White's and the Savoy, but as his relatives in the Robert Fleming family business noted, he had a tendency to recommend extremely risky investments, such as a silver mine in Bulgaria. But the managing partner of Rowe and Pitman, Lancy Smith, helped to introduce Ian to the intelligence world, for which Smith had done some work in the First World War. His brother, Aubrey, had served as deputy director of naval intelligence; another alumnus of the firm, Claud Serocold, had served as Private Secretary to Admiral 'Blinker' Hall.

In December 1935, to his mother's dismay, Peter Fleming, by then a very successful travel author, married the actress Celia Johnson. Ian also was snobbish but not about the beautiful Celia, rallying strongly to his brother's defence. Peter was, he said, one of the two or three most brilliant men of his generation. He must have enjoyed adding that no one could be expected to be perfect all the time. Celia Johnson went on to star in the wartime naval drama *In Which We Serve* and the iconic 1945 film, *Brief Encounter*.

Their mother returned to Turner House, obliging Ian to pursue his bachelor existence elsewhere. To general surprise, he did so by buying a decidedly peculiar flat on the upper floor of a house in unfashionable Ebury Street, close to Victoria.

The entrance had Doric columns, but the flat, albeit with a high ceiling, had no windows, only a skylight and wall lightings. A wall was covered with his by now impressive collection of first editions. Reflecting his real interest, more books were strewn around a table. Stairs led to a tiny bedroom and bathroom.

This archetypical bachelor pad was just large enough for a four at bridge with his male friends; its main purpose, though, was to entertain girls, who he tried to shock by inviting them to view his collection of French pornography. The writer Mary Pakenham was unimpressed. He affected, she said, to find women inferior, but if you were clever, 'You might occasionally manage to shoot one down.'

His future wife Ann O'Neill, on a first visit to him there, found him claiming to have a migraine and telling her to read a book for an hour 'until I am ready for you'. 'Considering the slightness of our acquaintance,' she found this 'very odd behaviour,' asking her diary, 'Why do I like cads and bounders?'

Prominent among his girlfriends in this period was Muriel Wright, a very pretty blonde who was a first class skier, rode to hounds and was a leading polo player. She also modelled country clothes and swimwear. Her Old Etonian father, with a vast estate in Derbyshire, had been an MP at the same time as his father. She adored Ian Fleming, getting herself described by unfriendly females as his slave. Her brother, enraged by Ian's treatment of his sister, arrived one day in Ebury Street with a horsewhip, only to find Fleming not at home. He was genuinely very fond of her but does not seem to have thought she was quite grand enough: her interests were in dogs and horses and his were not.

In 1938, while holidaying in Austria, he had spent time with Ann O'Neill, who had married her husband, Lord Shane O'Neill in 1932, when she was still nineteen. She already had embarked on an affair with Esmond Harmsworth, son of the newspaper proprietor, Lord Rothermere. Fleming's affair with her started early in 1939, apparently at a golf weekend in Sandwich, with neither of them taking it at all seriously.

Peter Fleming by now was working part time in military intelligence. Taking leave from Rowe and Pitman, with Peter's help, Ian got himself taken on by *The Times* to cover a trade mission to Moscow, but the talks made no progress. Ian had been recommended to Fitzroy Maclean at the British Embassy. When Maclean visited Ian at the Nacional Hotel, he found him in bed with a young lady from Odessa. Ian's conclusion was that the Soviet Union would be 'an exceedingly treacherous ally'. His memo on the subject earned him a meeting at the Foreign Office.

Ian Fleming also kept in touch with the Foreign Office about the rise and aggressive intentions of the Nazis, on which he regarded himself an expert. He wrote a long letter to *The Times* about it in September 1938. In March 1939, he visited Moscow with another trade mission, with his friend, Sefton Delmer of the *Daily Express*, producing a memorandum on the strength of the Russian Army and an anti-Bolshevik warning.

On a visit to Europe, he encountered Diana Napier, the wife of the tenor, Richard Tauber. He claimed to have bribed the steward to let him into her carriage, whereupon they made love to the 'hasty metal gallop of the wheels', a phrase he used in describing a similar episode in *From Russia, with Love*. He then told her that he did not want to see her again. As Mary Pakenham observed, this was the kind of episode Ian thought should be happening to him all the time.

CHAPTER XVII

FROM NAVAL
INTELLIGENCE TO
CASINO ROYALE

I n May 1939, Ian Fleming's amateur intelligence gathering earned a very important reward, as he was invited to lunch at the Carlton Grill with Admiral John Godfrey, recently appointed as director of naval intelligence. His predecessor, 'Blinker' Hall, had stressed to him the importance of getting a good personal assistant, as he had done with Claud Serocold. Godfrey consulted Montagu Norman, Governor of the Bank of England, who in turn consulted Serocold, Ian's former colleague at Rowe and Pitman, about finding a younger version of himself. It also may have helped that Norman's chief of staff had been Ian's boss at Reuters. Norman reported to Godfrey that he thought he had found the right man for him.

Wanting to 'have a good look at the fellow', Godfrey suggested that Ian should first come in part time. By July, he was appointed a lieutenant, soon to be commander in the Royal Naval Volunteer Reserve, then in August to naval intelligence, where he worked in the Admiralty in Room 39. Thrilled to have the three gold bands of a commander on his sleeve, he also had them added to the 'Turkish/ Balkan' cigarettes he chain-smoked and had made specially for him by Morlands.

Godfrey not only found him an excellent personal assistant but good at intelligence planning and willing to deal with everybody and everything Godfrey did not want to have to be bothered with. Godfrey had a reputation for being irascible in his dealings with other departments and left a lot of that to his deputy. For, according to Godfrey, that is what Fleming de facto became. He was closest to the Admiral, best at managing him and was kept in touch by him with all aspects of the work of the department. So the hitherto workshy Ian Fleming now was working long hours and enjoying it in a profession that suited him.

But at the outset, he had a lot to learn. He was reprimanded by Godfrey for taking two captured German U-boat officers to lunch at Scott's in a vain attempt to extract information from them! His idea of crashing a captured Heinkel airframe in the Channel in an effort to help the code breakers at Bletchley Park by 'pinching' an Enigma transmitter from German rescue vessels was ridiculed by the RAF. Most of the ideas in the 'Trout' memo of September 1939, which was circulated by Godfrey but written mainly by Fleming, were far-fetched and impractical, though idea No. 28 did find favour later as Operation Mincemeat.

When the Germans invaded Norway in April 1940, Peter Fleming led a six man team to Norway to help prepare for the despatch of a British force. He returned safely, despite having been reported as killed in an air raid.

In June, during the fall of France, Ian Fleming was sent there, to work with the British naval attaché in Paris and to try to liaise with Admiral Darlan, head of the French Navy, who had moved his headquarters west to Tours. It was not only Admiral Godfrey who wanted to know what Darlan proposed to do with the large French Mediterranean fleet, including two modern battleships.

In Paris, the Germans were expected on 14 June. On the 13th, Ian helped to secure the cash reserves of the MI6 team from a safe in the Rolls Royce company office and witnessed the burning of documents and closure of the embassy. He was unable to make any effective contact with Darlan before Darlan announced that he was joining Marshal Pétain's Vichy government, which was seeking an armistice with the Germans. Ian tried and failed to persuade the head of French signals intelligence to move to Britain with the Polish experts on Enigma.

Amidst the subsequent chaotic evacuation from Bordeaux, Fleming, with the MI6 representative Peter Smithers, bribed the harbour master to commandeer a ferry to take people to the British cruiser, HMS *Arethusa*. When it could take no more, they coerced several other small vessels into taking other escapees away. They burnt documents in the deserted consulate then attended a final dinner with the demoralised French at a restaurant where the proprietor opened his best wines, rather than serve them to the Germans. According to Smithers, in these chaotic circumstances, Ian Fleming remained completely calm. 'Nothing ruffled him in the least.' He then left for Portugal, via Spain. Meanwhile, Ian's younger brother Michael had been wounded and taken prisoner in the retreat to Dunkirk. In November, his family were informed that he had died of his wounds.

Ian Fleming's post war claim to have 'written the blue print' for the CIA used to be scoffed at by some of his friends, but it was at least partly true. For he made a serious contribution to doing so and was present at the creation of the Anglo-American intelligence relationship, which has endured ever since.

The still neutral United States did not have any central intelligence organisation. Ian Fleming came to revere, above all other intelligence chiefs, the wartime head of British Security Coordination in the United States, William Stephenson, who was determined not only to persuade the United States to set up a central intelligence agency but also to persuade the First World War veteran 'Wild Bill' Donovan to head it. As Ian Fleming wrote later, 'James Bond is a highly romanticised version of a real spy. The real thing is William Stephenson.'

In the very dark days of July 1940, Stephenson arranged for Donovan to visit Britain and for him to meet the King as well as Churchill and spend time with Admiral Godfrey. He also was introduced to the chiefs of staff. Donovan then helped to push through the agreement whereby the UK ceded bases in the Caribbean to the US in return for fifty destroyers. When Donovan later visited British bases in the Mediterranean, Ian Fleming was asked to brief him in Gibraltar on operation GOLDEN EYE, contingency planning to keep other sea routes open in case Gibraltar was threatened by Franco allying with the Germans.

In May 1941, in civilian clothes, Godfrey and Ian Fleming flew, via Lisbon, then the Azores and Bermuda to meet Stephenson in New York. In Lisbon, Ian had insisted on visiting the casino. Prefiguring Bond in *Casino Royale*, he said to Godfrey, 'What if the other players had been German spies and we had cleaned them out of their money?'

Ian found Stephenson to be a man of few words and 'panther like energy', with a love at the end of the day for strong martinis. In Washington, Godfrey and Ian started by paying their respects to Hoover, who was polite but uninterested in a naval mission. They were shown the FBI laboratory and shooting range. Stephenson's contacts arranged for Godfrey to be invited to a dinner with Mrs Roosevelt, at which her husband was bound to be present. Roosevelt asked some tough questions, but Godfrey was able to make the case for a central intelligence agency under Donovan. Two weeks later, Roosevelt announced Donovan's appointment as 'Coordinator of Information', creating the department that then morphed into the Office of Strategic Services (OSS) – the culmination of Stephenson's efforts, not those of Godfrey.

Having been impressed by how well he got on with the Americans, Godfrey left Ian behind for two months in Washington to help Donovan draw up the proposals for the new agency. Described by a female member of the embassy as 'looking simply smashing in his naval uniform', Ian discussed books with Isaiah Berlin and, for several weeks, occupied a bed in Donovan's Georgetown house while he wrote memoranda, the main theme of which was the advantages of close cooperation with and assistance from the British in getting the new organisation operational. Other passages did provide ideas for the OSS and a description of the type of leader it would require, which Allen Dulles later claimed had helped him to become head of the CIA! Donovan was said to have given Ian a .38 Police Colt revolver inscribed 'For Special Services', though this has never been traced since.

Back in London, he now came up with the idea that a special force was needed to act alongside frontline troops specifically to capture important intelligence targets. A small team of this kind was included in the disastrous raid on Dieppe. Ian was banned from going ashore by Godfrey but wrote an atmospheric account of the raid from an accompanying destroyer: 'The night was warm and still, and the red, green and white tracer in the distance seemed undangerous and even friendly.'

Such a unit now was formed, initially as a small commando team then as 30 Assault Unit. During the landings in North Africa, the head of the unit seized from American troops, who did not know what it was, an Enigma machine, which was sent post haste to Bletchley Park. They found another in the landings on Sicily.

To Ian's dismay, Godfrey was replaced in September 1942. Twice during 1943, Ian travelled across the Atlantic for Churchill/Roosevelt conferences, first the Trident conference in Washington in May then the Quebec conference in August. He also attended their conference in Cairo in November.

In the run up to the invasion of Sicily, Ian's colleague in Room 39, Ewen Montagu, helped to execute Operation Mincemeat. The 'Trout' memo had emphasised the art and importance of deception, likened to landing a fly on the nose of a trout. Amidst other eccentric ideas, the memo highlighted a suggestion in a book by Basil Thomson that a corpse dressed as an airman, with despatches in his pockets, could be deposited on the coast, supposedly from a parachute that had failed. 'I understand there is no difficulty obtaining corpses from the Naval Hospital, but, of course, it would have to be a fresh one!'

Before the Allied landings in Sicily in July 1943, a suitable corpse was located. It was equipped with the false identity of a major in the Marines, with a photo of and letters from his supposed girlfriend, plus other personal documents. The key item was a briefcase, chained to the corpse's wrist, containing a letter from Lieutenant-General Nye of the general staff to General Alexander specifying Greece and Crete as the real targets for invasion, with Sicily as the cover story.

Churchill having approved the operation, on 30 April a submarine was used to deposit the corpse in Southern Spain at Huelva, where German agents were known to be active. The Abwehr did get hold of the letter and a German signal decrypted on 14 May warned that the invasion was to be in the Balkans and this duly was reported to Churchill. After the war, in 1956, Ewen Montagu's account of the operation was made into a successful film: *The Man Who Never Was.*

While this had been a successful deception operation, it was not the main reason for the dispersal of German forces. For the fly had landed on the noses of Germans predisposed to swallow it. When Hitler met him in Rome, Mussolini forecast an invasion of Sicily, but Hitler expected an attack in the Balkans, as that was his conviction anyway. When the invasion went ahead in July, Sicily was occupied relatively easily, compared with the much tougher fighting thereafter in Italy.

During the Blitz, Ian Fleming had two lucky escapes. First when a bomb fell on Lincoln's Inn, where he was having dinner with Sefton Delmer. He then had an even closer shave, when another fell on the Carlton Hotel, where he was staying. But in March 1944, Muriel Wright, his girlfriend of nine years, was killed in a bombing raid.

He had got her a job as a despatch rider for the Admiralty. She was an immensely popular and very attractive figure, whizzing around London in her WRNS uniform on her motorbike, oblivious to the Blitz. Few of Ian's friends could understand why he did not marry her. He now had to identify her, still in her nightdress. Consumed by grief and guilt, he became very sentimental about her, with serious regret and remorse, declaring that 'she leaves a gap in my life that can never be filled'. His mistress, Ann Rothermere, worried that he might never get her out of his mind.

By the time of the Normandy invasion, the intelligence gathering unit dreamed up by Ian had become more than four hundred strong. Its officers became irritated by Ian's patronising manner and habit of referring to the unit as *his* 'Red Indians'. They had little time for their founder, who they regarded as a Whitehall warrior who did not participate in the risks they were taking. Some of the personnel proved unruly, particularly where women were concerned, causing Admiral Cunningham to start describing them as the 'Indecent Assault Unit'.

Ian was infuriated when, in Normandy, they were used for a conventional assault on Cherbourg, rather than for attempted intelligence gathering. Ian was sidelined when the expanded unit was placed under the control of a Marine Corps colonel. They continued, however, to carry out the kind of missions Fleming had envisaged for them. Near the end of the war, the test pilot Eric Brown described capturing in Kiel advanced German rocket components and the engineers who had devised them.

While in Normandy, Ian Fleming told a friend that, after the war, he was going to write 'the spy story to end all spy stories'. He also talked about not spending any more cold winters in England; he intended in future to spend them in Jamaica. After making a round the world visit of naval intelligence stations, he found that Ann's husband had been killed in action in Italy. Ann claimed to feel that his death had been a form of revenge on her, as making her cheating on him even more scandalous. Somerset Maugham agreed, saying that her conduct would have caused her to be ostracised not so long ago, but she could probably get away with it 'these days'.

Which proved to be the case as, still only thirty-two, Ann O'Neill had told Ian Fleming that she was planning to marry her long term lover, Esmond Harmsworth, now Lord Rothermere, owner of the *Daily Mail*. She claimed subsequently that she had hoped that Ian would dissuade her, but he made no attempt to do so. He did not want to get married and must also have felt that he could not afford her, and anyway, as she confessed, she wanted to become Lady Rothermere.

Both of them, however, firmly intended to continue their affair, which resumed immediately she got to New York, where they spent what they described as a four day 'honeymoon', while her husband flew on to Canada. Back in London, Ian rented accommodation within striking distance of her. Ann quickly started trying to interfere in the newspaper, while Ian continued playing golf and dining with his friend and her husband, Esmond.

He left naval intelligence intending to build the planned house in Jamaica, write a book and find a job that would permit him to do so. So he jumped at the chance when Lord Kemsley offered him an extremely generous salary and expenses to work as 'foreign manager' (not editor) for Kemsley Newspapers. The foreign correspondents he recruited included, in Washington, the Czech born Henry Brandon, who, until he got married, put Ian Fleming down as his next of kin. Another was the Australian Far East expert Richard Hughes, who featured as a character in *You Only Live Twice*. Several of them, including Brandon and Hughes, were part time helpers of MI6, now reverting to the name SIS (the Secret Intelligence Service). These associations were actively encouraged by Ian Fleming, who kept up such contacts himself and saw himself as 'running a world-wide intelligence organisation'! As part of his constant attempts to brighten up the paper, he hired Nancy Mitford to write a weekly column.

After his second wartime visit to Washington with Admiral Godfrey, Ian Fleming had visited Jamaica with his friend Ivar Bryce, who had a house on the island. It was Ivar Bryce who now found him a fifteen acre site with a small beach in Jamaica on which to build Goldeneye, named after the wartime operation. Maud Russell financed the purchase for him. He refused to install any windows, arranging instead louvred shutters, the better to enjoy the sea breezes. Thereafter he would spend hours snorkelling off the beach to admire the marine life nearby, leading him into an association with and great admiration for the French underwater explorer Jacques Cousteau.

In January 1948, Ann joined him at Goldeneye. Ian bought a book about the birds of the West Indies, the author of which was called James Bond, a name he found sufficiently masculine sounding to be worth bestowing on his future hero.

While he continued romances with attractive women, like the ultra rich American socialite Millicent Rogers and the writer Rosamond Lehmann, he was impressed by Ann's glamour, intelligence and social status, placing her in a different category. She spent long periods, several weeks at a time, every year, with him at

Goldeneye, pretending to her husband that she was there mainly to see Ian's friend and neighbour Noël Coward.

But, eventually, she warned him that 'Esmond is not going to tolerate us any more. It [their affair] is all over London,' partly because she could not resist gossiping about it herself. It was an extremely passionate relationship throughout the period in which it remained illicit. During it, she had written, 'I long for you even if you whip me,' so long as she was kissed afterwards. He reciprocated by promising that after the next time they met, she wouldn't be able to sit down for a while. Other notes from her included, 'It's very lonely not to be beaten and shouted at every five minutes and contradicted all the time', even though he was usually wrong. In 1948, she had a baby girl with Fleming while still married to Rothermere, though the child died shortly after being born.

When Ian Fleming finally married Ann Rothermere in 1952, they had been lovers for fifteen years. Having caused her divorce and with Ann pregnant by then with their son Caspar, Fleming had to resign himself to marriage, an institution for which he had never previously been able to see 'what's in it for me?' His friends believed that Ann had engaged in some deliberate entrapment. As the final nail in Ian's life as a bachelor, Rothermere complained about Ian's conduct to his fellow proprietor, Lord Kemsley, who told Ian, who was heading for Jamaica, that he had better come back married, or not at all. What he described as his 'supposedly carefree existence' was about to come to an end.

Ever afterwards, Ian claimed that he started writing *Casino Royale* to take his mind off marriage. He now had to provide for a woman who was used to being very rich and entertaining lavishly, though she received a £100,000 divorce settlement.

In March 1952, they got married very happily at the Town Hall in Jamaica, with Noël Coward attending, with some verses for them, ending that they could not be accused of having got married in haste! Ann noted approvingly that Ian had started to write *Casino Royale*, beginning with the words, 'The scent and smoke and sweat of a casino are nauseating at three in the morning.'

But Ann Fleming observed that Ian was 'completely egocentric'. He wanted to have an interesting and exciting life, and nothing else mattered.

Almost exactly the same could have been, and was, said about her. Antonia Fraser concluded that her main interest was herself. Others described her as hard as nails. Ian was told, from the outset, that she could not live without 'society', by which she meant the innumerable lunches and soirées she held for her very select circle of friends.

She had been used to entertaining on a grand scale as Lady Rothermere. To enable her to continue to do so, more modestly but still very expensively, he bought them a house in Victoria Square, close enough to Parliament to be able to attract interesting MPs. Wearing glamorous off the shoulder gowns, she revelled in continuing her never ending entertainment of her society friends. Members of what Ian described as her harem included Lucian Freud, spotted on one occasion eating a bunch of orchids, Diana Cooper, Loelia Westminster, Evelyn Waugh, Randolph Churchill, Cyril Connolly, Peter Quennell, Cecil Beaton and an array of other literary and artistic luminaries, many of whom Ian could not stand.

There was a period when they still got on pretty well together and there were many others when they vowed to stop alienating and hurting one another. But marriage quite soon seemed to dampen what, so long as it remained illicit, had been a consuming passion. She had a difficult pregnancy and even more difficult birth of their son. Two Caesarean sections had left her with major scars that Fleming found off-putting. They led increasingly separate lives. She hated flying and Fleming banned her from joining him at Goldeneye until Caspar was older. The physical relationship had broken down. 'You mention "bad old bachelor days",' she complained. Since they got married, 'The only person you stopped sleeping with was me!'

In September 1955, the Flemings had been invited to lunch at Chequers with the Prime Minister, Anthony Eden. Ian Fleming was not a fan of Eden, but Ann knew his wife, Clarissa. On 7 November 1956, an ailing Anthony Eden was forced by US pressure and his Cabinet colleagues to end his attempt to occupy the Suez Canal Zone. Given Eden's exhaustion and need for complete rest, his minister of state, Alan Lennox-Boyd, asked Ian Fleming if Eden and his wife could recuperate for a month at Goldeneye.

They arrived on 24 November. Neither Ian nor Ann were there. So the arrangements were made, extra telephones were installed, extra servants were hired and the house and garden were spruced up by the wife of the Governor, Sir Hugh Foot, and Ian's friend and neighbour, an attractive divorcée called Blanche Blackwell, who loved swimming off his beach. The Edens had been warned that the house and estate were quite primitive, but they barely ventured out of the gates as they loved the peaceful time they had there. The Prime Minister's retreat to Goldeneye put the final nail in his political coffin. On his return, he was replaced by Harold Macmillan. Blanche Blackwell's involvement in helping with the visit infuriated Ann Fleming.

In November 1956, while Eden was recuperating at Goldeneye, Ann embarked in Paris on her six year affair with the highly
intelligent and impressive Hugh Gaitskell, who looked likely to
become the next Prime Minister. He was not at all good looking
and seemed rather desiccated. As they borrowed the apartment of
Anthony Crosland, Ann claimed that she used to imagine she was
making love to the much better looking Crosland. But Gaitskell
loved dancing, twirling her around at the Café Royal. She claimed
to have introduced him to 'wine, women and song', the 'women'
being her.

When she reappeared at Goldeneye, this did not prevent her
flying into a furious rage about the role Blanche Blackwell had
played in looking after the Edens. A garden Blanche had planted
was torn up by her. She was accused of having an affair with Ian,
which was not yet the case. Pretty soon thereafter, Ian Fleming did
begin his affair with Blanche Blackwell, who he found 'a lot more
fun' than Ann. Ann started referring to her as his 'black woman', as
if she were of mixed race.

Although he affected to be unconcerned about her 'fling' with
Gaitskell, in reality, Fleming resented it bitterly, as she was famously
indiscreet and it was so well known to all their friends. At a dinner
he attended at the US Embassy, he was asked by a guest who was
the person at the end of the table. 'That's Hugh Gaitskell, my wife's
lover,' he replied, loudly. Hitherto regarded as a great Don Juan, he
was not enjoying the role of a cuckolded husband.

But he did enjoy the episode when, to meet Ann, Gaitskell appeared in Jamaica on a 'fact finding mission'. Despite an appeal from
Ann to Beaverbrook to call him off, the local *Daily Express* stringer,
having heard rumours of their affair, pursued Gaitskell, causing

him to drive off in a panic in his car, leaving Ann behind. When she arrived dishevelled, having had to walk back to Goldeneye, Ian Fleming found it hilarious that her tryst with Gaitskell had gone so awry, offering to challenge him to a duel for having left her on her own at the mercy of the locals. Ann lamented to Diana Cooper that the gold had gone from Goldeneye, but she still loved Ian. 'Isn't it odd?' She added.

In London, after dinner at Boodle's, Ian would head for his bedroom in Victoria Square, bypassing Ann's gossipy soirées. Nevertheless, amidst one of their efforts to reconcile, to enable her to entertain also in the country, he ended up buying her a vast country house at Sevenhampton, far from the sea and his favourite golf courses, which then required four years not just of renovation but of rebuilding. The project was a hugely expensive fiasco. When asked how his marriage was going, Ian Fleming replied, 'As well as I deserve.' As he pursued his efforts to sell and win TV and film rights for his books, they were spending less and less time together.

'In the present twilight,' he wrote, 'we are hurting each other to an extent that makes life hardly bearable.' He loved Goldeneye and writing his Bond books; she concentrated on her successful salon in London. Somerset Maugham congratulated her on her skill in taming and civilising Labour politicians – justifiably as, post Gaitskell and Ian, she had an affair also with Roy Jenkins.

In 1961, in the midst of what he found the very stressful legal dispute over the authorship of *Thunderball*, Ian Fleming suffered a massive heart attack while attending a meeting at the *Sunday Times*. He spent a month in the London Clinic, followed by convalescing at a hotel by the sea in Hove. During his recovery, he wrote the children's novel *Chitty Chitty Bang Bang*, based on the bedtime stories he told his son Caspar about two magical cars. Sadly, he remained thereafter an invalid, experiencing frequent chest pains and shortness of breath. Congratulated on his, soon thereafter, spectacular success, he said that he would give it all up for a healthy heart. Yet, to the despair of his doctors, he flatly refused to give up drinking or smoking until he died.

On 8 August 1964, he was thrilled to be nominated as club captain for the following year at his favourite golf club, the Royal St George. On the 11th, he suffered a further heart attack while still staying at Sandwich. His last words were to the ambulance drivers were, 'I am sorry to trouble you, chaps. I don't know how you get along so fast with the traffic on the roads these days.' He died in Canterbury hospital that night.

At the private funeral, in the parish church at Sevenhampton, his wife arrived late, causing the service to have to be restarted. When, after his death, Blanche Blackwell claimed to have been Ian Fleming's 'true love', which, towards the end, she was, Rebecca West observed that the number of women who believed that to be the case 'would fill the Albert Hall, bless his heart'.

In Ian Fleming's last novel, though looking forward to a holiday with the delicious Miss Goodnight, Bond had concluded that 'love from her, or from any other woman, was not enough for him'. It would be like taking 'a room with a view'. For James Bond, the same view would always pall.

This was the way Ian Fleming lived most of his life until his marriage, through the early years of which he did try to behave better. Yet the 'Me Too' movement would have struggled with how to deal with him, for all his 'conquests' were volunteers. There is no record of any female complaints about being harassed by him. In both his looks and character, he was extremely attractive to women, who seemed even to appreciate his periodic fits of loneliness and, later, melancholy.

Before he died, Ian Fleming received awards from Pan for having sold one million books. The figure today is estimated to be over a hundred million. They remain defiantly in print, while those of his critics have long since disappeared.

CHAPTER XVIII

THE BOND PHENOMENON

'Bond is what every man would like to be and what every woman
would like between her sheets. But only in their daydreams.'
RAYMOND MORTIMER

'The cinema was a lot less fun before 007.'
DILYS POWELL, *SUNDAY TIMES*

During the war, Ian Fleming had said that he intended to write 'the spy novel to end all spy novels'. Years later, when his brother Peter was writing another of his successful travel books, Ian had asked him why, instead, he did not write a bestseller. 'It's not so easy,' was Peter Fleming's reply. Ian bet him a hundred pounds that he could write one. In 1951, Peter Fleming did try his hand at a spy novel, *The Sixth Column*, before reverting to his far more successful travel writing.

Ian Fleming's confidence came from his conviction that there was and had been plenty of thriller material in his own life. As his biographer, Nicholas Shakespeare, observed, there would have been no James Bond had Ian Fleming not lived the life he did. When at last he began to write *Casino Royale*, which he completed in eight weeks, he sought to incorporate as many as possible of his own experiences, amidst all the venues and exotic locations he had frequented.

The defining period of Ian Fleming's life had been the war. He was intensely proud of Britain's role in it and of his own contribution to it and to the US alliance. As a staff officer, he had not been required to engage in combat himself, but in the special forces and the combat units, he knew or knew about plenty of his comrades who had engaged in displays of derring-do no less dramatic than those of Bond.

The first and by far the most important thing he had to do was to establish the *persona* of his main character, which was not too difficult, as he intended to base it on an enhanced version of himself. Bond is introduced as extremely good looking, though with something cold and ruthless in his eyes. He drives a supercharged version of a powerful Bentley, drinks Martinis which must be shaken, not stirred. He smokes Fleming's favourite Morland cigarettes from the same gunmetal cigarette case. The epitome of Fleming's version of Englishness, he is passionate about golf and a devotee of London clubland. They have the same attitude and appeal to women; Ian Fleming had just as many girlfriends as Bond. Both are connoisseurs of casinos. What better venue, therefore, could there be for Bond's first showdown with the villainous Le Chiffre?

This version of Ian Fleming carries a flat .25 Beretta under his dinner jacket since, as 007 in the Secret Service, he is licenced to kill – an inspired invention by Fleming, investing his hero with a special aura and appeal. Other action heroes might do some killing, but they were not explicitly authorised to do so.

He has been chosen for this mission as the best card player in the service. His assistant, Vesper, assigned to him by French intelligence, is wearing a simple black couture dress and 'a diamond clip in the low vee which just exposed the jutting swell of her breasts' (a feature of all Bond heroines). Sharing Fleming's attitude to women, and it being imperative to keep him free for a different entanglement in every story, Bond has no time for lengthy seductions and claims to be cynical about affairs – 'the touch of the hand, the kiss, the passionate kiss, the feel of the body, the climax in the bed, then more bed, then less bed,' then tears and final bitterness.

Casino Royale brought together the worlds of gambling and espionage, both of which Fleming knew well. Its most memorable scenes were those of the battle in the Casino between Bond and the evil Le Chiffre, who had cheated his Russian paymasters. To prevail, Bond, on the verge of disaster, has to borrow funds from his CIA colleague Felix Leiter. But Vesper (apparently) is abducted and Bond, trying to rescue her, is captured by Le Chiffre. There follows a torture passage, with Bond's private parts being flayed with a cane carpet beater. Ironically, this, the most sadistic passage in the Bond books, was at Bond's expense. Unexpectedly, Le Chiffre then is disposed of by an agent of the Russian 'death to spies' organisation, SMERSH. This supposed invention by Ian Fleming was based on reality, then and now.

Having advertised his belief only in short term relationships, Bond falls at the first hurdle. Enjoying a torrid affair with the beautiful Vesper, he decides to marry her, but far from getting the girl, at the very point he decides to do so, she confesses to have been working for the Russians, having betrayed not only him to Le Chiffre but other Western intelligence operations as well. As she commits suicide, the story ends brutally with, 'The bitch is dead now,' not accepting that she was caught in a trap she could not escape. *Casino Royale* was not only a spy novel; it also was the story of a tragic love affair.

Apart from the bizarre torture scene, Fleming made a more amusing mistake, subsequently having to disavow Bond's dire recipe for martinis, nowadays portrayed as a Vesper martini, which entailed mixing gin and vodka, not one or the other, plus the quinine based kina lillet, which no longer exists. Shaken not stirred, however, does improve the presentation, though not the taste.

When he showed the manuscript to his friend, William Plomer, who worked at the publishers Jonathan Cape, a much less confident Fleming was far from sure that it was good enough to publish. Plomer showed it to a colleague, who stayed up late reading it and wanted more of the same. The editorial director was horrified by the sadistic violence and did not want to be associated with it. Yet, given the readability of the rest of the story, Cape agreed to publish it and, potentially, his next book.

William Plomer had advised Ian that it was no use writing just one book of the kind he had in mind. He must aim for a series, drilling his themes and characterisations into the heads of the potential public.

The reviews, some of them from Fleming's contacts, were enthusiastic, with his friends at the *Sunday Times* commending his 'startlingly vivid turn of phrase.' *The Observer* advised, 'Don't miss this.' There were comparisons with Eric Ambler and Peter Cheyney.

A critic who found the plot 'staggeringly implausible', still found the book exciting. John Betjeman admired the author's ability 'to work up to a climax unrevealed at the end of each chapter.' Those who bought the book liked it. It had several print runs and his publisher announced that a copy was being sold every six minutes the bookshops were open.

Fleming failed in his strenuous efforts to get the book filmed, though CBS produced a TV version with the excellent Peter Lorre as Le Chiffre and there was an American version of the book, entitled *You Asked for It*, with a barely dressed girl on the cover.

In 1967, a spoof Bond film entitled *Casino Royale* appeared with David Niven as the hero in a very lame parody. It was not until 2006 that a first rate film was made of *Casino Royale*, with Eva Green as Vesper and Daniel Craig as a new sharp edged Bond.

Ian Fleming's second novel, *Live and Let Die*, featured the hoodlum drug baron Mr Big, the voodoo practising villain Bond encounters in Harlem, and the tarot card reading Solitaire, who can read the future so long as she remains a virgin, which, as she falls for Bond, she does not. With Fleming doing his own research in Harlem, the action then moved to Florida and the Bahamas. In Florida, Bond's CIA friend Felix Leiter barely survives being thrown into a shark tank, with a note left stating, 'He disagreed with something that ate him.'

While at the *Sunday Times*, Ian had written a book called *Thrilling Cities* and, thereafter, he painstakingly researched any venue he did not know already, increasing the atmospheric authenticity of his stories and enabling him to claim never to have written about places he hadn't seen.

The *Sunday Times* reviewer loyally observed 'how wincingly well

Mr Fleming writes'. The *Evening Standard* found the book 'tense, ice cold, sophisticated'. Raymond Chandler was impressed by the scenes in Harlem. The fact that it was banned in Ireland for salaciousness helped with sales in Britain, but in the US, to his great disappointment, only five thousand copies were sold.

Ian Fleming himself agreed several changes to the US edition, eliminating the n-word and 'honky', which he regarded as Harlem speech. The night club audience there, watching a near naked girl dancer, were no longer portrayed as 'panting and grunting like pigs at a trough'; instead, Bond 'could sense the electric tension in the room'.

Live and Let Die very clearly was written in the hope and expectation that it would be filmed. It was a bitter disappointment to Ian Fleming that nothing came of this when he published it, with Hollywood studios finding his stories 'too British' and 'too sexual'.

In his third novel, *Moonraker*, Sir Hugo Drax, by now a pillar of the British business establishment, had been found as a boy, suffering from amnesia, on a battlefield in the Ardennes. But Bond is called in because he cheats at cards in his club. Drax turns out to be a former German *werewolf* (a resistance force intended to work behind Allied lines in the war), working with fellow Germans on a nuclear rocket to destroy London. Bond saves the day but does not get his expected reward, as his female partner with 'jutting breasts' gets married instead. Published in 1955, *The Observer* described *Moonraker* as 'irresistibly readable, however incredible'.

The book was not Fleming's best and he was discouraged by the reaction to it. His wife, Ann, and her pretentious circle did not take Ian's lowbrow novels seriously at all. She had refused to have *Casino Royale* dedicated to her, finding it way below her taste. Noël

Coward found the book 'far-fetched,' but 'I would so love him to triumph over the sneers of Annie's intellectual friends'.

Fleming was fascinated by the illegal diamond trade, which formed the subject of his next two books, *Diamonds Are Forever* and, one year later, the non-fiction *The Diamond Smugglers*. For these, he needed serious expertise, which was provided for him by the South African company Anglo American, which, through De Beers, controlled much of the world's legitimate diamond trade. Two of his friends were senior executives there and Anglo had appointed Sir Percy Sillitoe, former head of MI5, to help them combat diamond smuggling.

During his war service and thereafter, Fleming also had spent time with experts in what he described as 'gadgets and gimmicks'. Robert Churchill, a gunsmith, showed him a gas pistol disguised as a fountain pen, with two kinds of cartridges, one lethal, one nonlethal. But Fleming's main source was Charles Fraser-Smith, an official in the Ministry of Supply who was the quartermaster to MI6. He showed him shaving brushes with secret cavities, shoelaces that could act as saws and hollowed out golf balls to conceal messages to prisoners of war, a device Fleming used for the smuggling of uncut stones in *Diamonds Are Forever*.

Geoffrey Boothroyd, a firearms expert, persuaded him that Bond would have to give up his .32 Beretta, which he described as a 'ladies' gun', with no real stopping power. So, in *Dr. No*, a reluctant Bond is ordered by 'M' to switch to a Walther PPK. Fraser-Smith featured as 'Boothroyd' in the novels before the character was developed into the popular 'Q', played by Desmond Llewelyn in the Bond films.

Ian Fleming confessed to Evelyn Waugh that he was struggling with love scenes, some of which from his previous books had been ridiculed by his wife's friends. Raymond Chandler again urged him to 'aim higher'. Fleming replied that his books were straightforward fantasies 'of the bang-bang, kiss-kiss variety', and he was not aiming any higher than that.

His novels were based on a fantastic representation of the life of action he never had as a staff officer in intelligence. They were escapist novels, at a time when Britain still was suffering from post war austerity. Credibility was enhanced by the mass of detail he provided for every striking scene.

Fleming was exploiting situations that did exist, like the Cold War, the struggle within it between MI6 and the KGB and the fight against organised crime. Invariably, he included large swathes of factual background and atmosphere, of places and personal experiences, to provide an air of authenticity. But, as he explained, *he was not looking for stories that people could believe in, but for ones sufficiently fantastic and exciting to command a temporary suspension of disbelief* in the interest of wanting to know what happened next. Hence his surprise at the raft of critics who claimed to see in them some sort of objectionable social statement.

Somerset Maugham was impressed by Ian's ability 'to get the tension to the highest pitch'. The reviews were favourable, as demonstrating Fleming and Bond's 'staying power'. But there were concerns about its 'salaciousness', with Tiffany, at the end the of the book, urging Bond to do whatever he wanted to her, 'Now!'

Having written four novels, Ian Fleming had achieved numerous reprints and successful sales, but as yet, he had made very little money from them. In the US, the chief critic of the *New York Times* was a relentless opponent. Film offers had kept coming then petering out. He was close to despairing about the feeble American sales.

All of which had caused him an untypical phase of self-doubt as he worked on the manuscript of his next book. He told friends that he was thinking of killing off his hero, a threat not to be taken too seriously, as Bond was his alter ego. This turned out to be precisely the point at which, following the publication of *Diamonds Are Forever*, Bond was becoming a cult figure. Sales had taken off in both Britain and the United States and there followed, in 1957, a knockout success with *From Russia, with Love*.

Fleming, who spoke some Russian, knew plenty about the Soviet system and its espionage organisations, including having witnessed the prosecutor Vyshinsky at the Vickers trial and from his time in naval intelligence.

Bond is lured to Istanbul by a beautiful Russian girl claiming to want to defect. Her boss is a memorable villainess, the unspeakably ugly and evil SMERSH operative Colonel Rosa Klebb. He finds Tatiana in his hotel room wearing only a black ribbon around her neck. On the Orient Express back to London he is fooled by a pretend colleague sent to help him. Bond uses his reinforced metal cigarette case to stop a bullet fired direct at his heart. But, at the end, Rosa Klebb manages to kick Bond with a poisoned dagger hidden in her boot, leaving him lying crumpled on the floor, with uncertainty as to whether he would recover.

Ian Fleming regarded it as his best book. As sales took off, this was not the moment to dispose of his hero. It was announced that a notice had been posted at Secret Service headquarters stating that Bond was recovering from severe Fugu curare poisoning, with the toxin made from the glands of the Japanese globefish!

The book sold out immediately and was serialised in the *Daily*

Express. In March 1960, Fleming had met the then Senator Kennedy at a dinner in Georgetown. Kennedy already had read two of his books, circulated by the *Sunday Times* correspondent Fleming had sent to Washington, Henry Brandon. Brandon told him that the entire Kennedy family were reading his books. *From Russia, with Love* was given a huge boost by being included in the published list of the by now President Kennedy's ten favourite books. Having struggled hitherto in the US market, Ian Fleming now was telling his American publisher that he intended to write 'the same book, over and over again'!

Jackie Kennedy gave a copy to Allen Dulles, head of the CIA, who had sought out Ian Fleming in London a few weeks before. Dulles's biographer recalled that in his wartime memo to Donovan, Fleming had advised that the head of the new US intelligence agency must be a man of 'the utmost discretion, sobriety, devotion to duty' and wide experience, which Dulles claimed was the template for his appointment. On publishing his book, *The Craft of Intelligence*, after being ousted as director of the CIA following the Bay of Pigs fiasco in Cuba, Dulles claimed that what the agency needed was 'half a dozen James Bonds'!

Bond by now had even attracted attention in Moscow. In May 1962, the Soviet journal *Izvestia* warned that he was the invention of a 'retired spy' who was a friend of Allen Dulles. By this stage, his novels had been or were being translated into eighteen languages.

His next story, *Dr. No*, started with the assassination of the MI6 representative in Jamaica, who had been investigating the activities of Dr No on a remote island called Crab Key. Bond avoids the poisoned fruit in his room and deadly centipede in his bed. With his Jamaican friend, Quarrel, he meets a beautiful shell collector,

Honey Ryder. Quarrel is killed by the pretend local dragon, a flame throwing buggy. Dr No has plans to disrupt US missile tests. Having survived extended capture and torture, Bond buries Dr No under a consignment of his own guano fertiliser.

Despite his war service, Ian's affairs and the 'salaciousness' of his novels caused some of the staider Flemings to worry about his reputation. His brother Richard, war hero and head of the family bank, was sufficiently concerned for his wife to be obliged, on a flight to the US, to devour *The Spy Who Loved Me* wrapped in a brown paper cover.

On the publication of *Dr. No*, which contained no questionable passages, Fleming was surprised to find himself the subject of a concerted attack by critics. A Professor Bernard Bergonzi attacked Bond's snobbery, salaciousness and the fantasies of upper class life intended (he shrewdly suspected) to compensate for the rigours of life in the post war welfare state. In the *New Statesman*, Paul Johnson followed up with an article entitled 'Sex, Snobbery and Sadism', describing *Dr. No* as the nastiest book he had ever read, combining the sadism of a school bully, the sex longings of a frustrated adolescent and the snob cravings of a suburban adult. 'Mr Fleming has no literary skill,' he claimed. The plot was incredible and chaotic. It was a dish fit only to be served up in a Lyons Corner House (a curiously snobbish observation). *The Guardian* followed suit; *The Times* declared that the Bond books were most professional but their appeal had 'its much nastier side'.

Ian Fleming felt that he was being accused of snobbery by a cohort of pretentious, self styled intellectual snobs. He was used to his efforts being looked down upon by highbrow critics convinced, contrary to the evidence and his readers' response, that he couldn't write. Some of his characterisations, especially of his villains, were superb. His plots, however far-fetched, always were inventive.

It anyway was far too late to stop Bond taking off into an orbit from which he has yet to return. *Dr. No* originally had been conceived by Fleming as a screenplay and this time the film offer was for real. In 1961, the American Albert ('Cubby') Broccoli and Canadian Harry Saltzman, both wanting to make films at the Pinewood Studios outside London, formed Eon Productions to film the Bond stories. They raised the $1 million to make the first, low budget Bond film.

When Ian signed the film agreement with Cubby Broccoli, a decimal point was in the wrong place, meaning that he would have received only miserly profits from the films. Broccoli sent it back to him, inviting him to correct it! It was the enthusiastic and dynamic sponsorship of Cubby Broccoli that launched James Bond into orbit.

Fleming had doubts about the choice of Sean Connery as Bond. He had hoped for Richard Burton or Roger Moore. On meeting him, Fleming felt that Connery was not his idea of Bond at all. He wanted an upper class Bond, not a Glasgow 'roughneck' who he doubted would have the 'social grace' to play his hero. As he soon acknowledged, his impression had been mistaken, as Connery proceeded to give Bond precisely the sharp edge Fleming had portrayed him as having beneath the suave exterior.

In this, the very first Bond film, the director, Terence Young, created the template for every Bond movie thereafter to open with a bang. For he introduced the gun barrel opening image of Bond walking past the camera, then turning to shoot, followed by a shower of blood, with the accompanying Bond music theme by

Monty Norman and John Barry. In *Dr. No*, memorably, this featured the three assassins with white sticks pretending to be blind, walking to the tune of 'Three Blind Mice' before killing the MI6 representative in Jamaica.

Richard Maibaum, who was mainly responsible for the screenplay of this and a dozen other Bond films, followed Fleming's story pretty closely, except that Dr No is disposed of in a nuclear reactor rather than under a pile of fertiliser. With Caribbean locations, and who can forget Ursula Andress emerging from the ocean with a knife in her bikini, the film became a cult movie from day one. Andress set the template for a Bond female of being not just gorgeous but tough and resourceful as well. Fleming met Sean Connery and Ursula Andress on the set of *Dr. No* and attended the triumphal premiere.

Top secret at the time was the fact that Sean Connery, being very prematurely bald, had to wear a hairpiece in all his Bond movies, glued on extra firmly for the action scenes. The only minor sign of on screen slippage was in the underwater scenes of *You Only Live Twice*. Ursula Andress's voice had to be dubbed over in *Dr. No* because of her heavy Swiss German accent, none of which has prevented Sean Connery to this day being rated the best ever Bond and Andress the best ever Bond girl.

So by the end of 1963, Fleming had achieved his dream of huge commercial success. Sales of *Dr. No* and *From Russia, with Love* were approaching one million each, soon to be overtaken by seven million sales in paperback in the United States. Yet by this time, due above all to his failing health but also the state of his marriage, he was far from being able to enjoy the extent of his success, which immediately was further enhanced by the next blockbuster Bond movie of *From Russia, With Love*, with Tatiana played by Daniela Bianchi.

In the film, Bond realises that the colleague sent to help him is a fraud when he orders red wine with his fish! But several scenes are stolen by the villainous Dr Klebb, played by Lotte Lenya, the wife of Kurt Weill and star of *The Threepenny Opera*. At the end, ordered by Klebb to shoot Bond, Tatiana shoots Klebb instead.

Ian Fleming attended the premiere of *From Russia, with Love* at the London Pavilion in October, appearing alarmingly frail and with his doctor in attendance. He provided a vast amount of caviar for the party held by Ann afterwards but barely participated in it himself.

Sadly, he died five weeks before the premiere in 1964 of, arguably, the greatest of all Bond films, though he did visit the Pinewood set to meet Connery and the blonde Shirley Eaton who, in the film, perished coated with gold. His novel *Goldfinger* had raced to the top of the bestseller list, ahead of *Dr Zhivago*. The film combined an ingenious plot, improved in the screenplay by Richard Maibaum, two excellent villains in Goldfinger, played by Gert Fröbe, and Oddjob, and the unforgettable Honor Blackman with the unusual title of Pussy Galore. The vital change made by Maibaum was to have the defenders of Fort Knox disabled not by poisoned water but by a spray loosed from the planes of Pussy Galore's team of female pilots.

The opening battle of wits between Bond and Goldfinger at Fleming's favourite Royal Saint George's golf club culminated with Oddjob using the steel rim of his bowler hat to decapitate a statue and crushing a golf ball between his fingers. As a circular saw approached Bond's vital parts, the film contained the iconic exchange between Bond and Goldfinger:

'Do you expect me to talk?'

'No, Mr Bond, I expect you to die!'

Oddjob is electrocuted by Bond. Pussy Galore is converted from lesbianism because, she claimed, she had 'never met a man before'. The defenders of Fort Knox all pretend to be incapacitated by the knockout spray from her planes. Ever since, it has generally been regarded as the best of all Bond films, with *From Russia, with Love* and *Dr. No* frequently rated numbers two and three.

In his address at the memorial service for Ian Fleming, attended, among countless others, by Graham Greene, Evelyn Waugh and Isaiah Berlin, his friend and editor William Plomer said that 'although Ian Fleming's books had made him world famous, he was modest about them to the end ... He never pretended they were more than popular entertainments ... He was exposed to a lot of envy ... but never took much notice of it.' The best response to those who disapproved of Bond were the 'cheerful reactions' of the film audiences, who enjoyed not only the excitingly realistic detail but the whole romantic notion of a dragon slaying, maiden rescuing hero, which had enabled Ian Fleming to create a myth of such universal appeal. His adventures were something of an adolescent fantasy, but what was wrong with that? He was proud of how he composed them and never pretended that they were more than entertainment. Some found his books distasteful, 'but I have never heard them called boring'.

By the time Ian Fleming died, the criticism had become irrelevant, given the extraordinary popular and commercial success he had achieved. Anthony Burgess proved shrewder than his literary counterparts in concluding that 'Bond has the stuff of immortality in him'.

For there was far more yet to come, as his death did nothing to arrest the onward and upward progression of Bond. Nearly all Ian Fleming's Bond novels and short stories ended up as films, though some scarcely at all as written by him. There followed film after film that owed its success to the combination of inventiveness, brilliant cinematography and 'enhancements' plus, increasingly, some entirely new creations by the screenwriters, especially Richard Maibaum and Tom Mankiewicz.

Thunderball, published in 1961, had been intended to be the first Bond film. It was based on a screenplay on which Fleming had worked with Kevin McClory and Jack Whittingham. Its appearance was delayed by a legal dispute pursued relentlessly by McClory. This took a toll on Ian Fleming, obliging him to spend weeks on end in court. It was during the trial that Fleming suffered his first heart attack. His doctors tried in vain to stop him drinking and smoking, but, to the full extent he could, he had chosen to live as in his favourite Jack London quote, cited in *You Only Live Twice*, published in the year he died: 'The proper function of man is to live, not to exist. I shall not waste my days in trying to prolong them. I shall use my time.'

In the film, produced in 1965, Ernst Stavro Blofeld makes his first appearance as head of the international crime syndicate SPECTRE. With his deputy, the eyepatch wearing Emilio Largo, they have seized two nuclear bombs. A *femme fatale*, Fiona Volpe, is killed in Bond's arms when he twists her around to receive a bullet intended for him. Bond wins over Largo's mistress, Domino. Bond recovers the bombs and is saved from being shot by her.

While the plot was regarded as extremely far-fetched, the film got a good reception, helped by the spectacular locations in the

Bahamas and stunning, though overlong, underwater photography. It was a huge commercial success, earning an at that time stunning $140 million.

In the same year, Kingsley Amis published his homage to Fleming's creation in *The James Bond Dossier*, a critical analysis of Ian Fleming's writings that was seen as a 'two-fingered salute' to Fleming's critics. A huge Bond fan and defender of popular literature, Amis argued that Bond was not a spy but a counter-spy, that he was not an exploiter but a protector of women and that Fleming's stories had 'just as much in them' as more ambitious kinds of fiction. Amis was invited to write a follow up novel, which he entitled *Colonel Sun*, but only fragments from it were used in the subsequent Bond films.

In *You Only Live Twice*, Fleming's story was based on Bond's haiku like reflection that 'you only live twice. Once when you are born, and once when you look death in the face.'

In bad shape and having been drinking heavily, Bond is despatched on a mission to Japan. The Japanese intelligence chief, Tanaka, wants him to kill the evil leader of a cult on a remote island, who turns out to be Blofeld. After a duel, Bond strangles Blofeld and blows up his castle but is left, suffering from amnesia, in a Japanese fishing village with 'Kissy' Suzuki.

The book was denounced by Fleming's sometime friend Cyril Connolly as little more than a Japanese travelogue with no credible plot.

The 1967 film, with a screenplay by Roald Dahl, had a more ambitious story. Bond is sent to Japan because an American and then a Soviet spacecraft have been hijacked in an attempt to provoke a clash between them to benefit a third power, presumably China.

The organiser is Blofeld, from a base inside a volcano. Bond teams up with Tanaka and his ninjas to storm Blofeld's base and abort his spacecraft before it strikes its American target and starts a war.

The film was saved by the dramatic scenery and action scenes. An unhappy Sean Connery, required to adopt a Japanese disguise, vowed never to make another Bond film. The Queen attended the premiere, and it was a commercial success but with poor reviews.

When Fleming's novel *On Her Majesty's Secret Service* was published in 1963, it had been greeted with a sigh of relief as a return to form by him after the disaster of *The Spy Who Loved Me*. It got a positive reception, including in the US press, except from Anthony Boucher in the *New York Times* who, in disliking it, had lamented that 'you can't argue with success', having done his best not to take his own advice.

The 1969 film, closely based on the novel, followed Blofeld's plans to wage biological warfare against Britain with the aid of twenty brainwashed Bond girls. The story reflected Fleming's love of the Alps and carried with it strong echoes of Muriel Wright. Having defeated Blofeld, Bond decides to marry the troubled Tracy. But with their Aston Martin DB5 still bedecked with flowers, she is shot and killed by Blofeld's sidekick, the ghastly Irma Bunt.

While Diana Rigg was a great success as Tracy, it was never going to be easy to succeed Sean Connery, and George Lazenby struggled as Bond. The film fared poorly at the box office, with receipts falling to $64 million.

In the 1971 film of *Diamonds Are Forever*, therefore, Sean Connery had to be persuaded to return as Bond. Shirley Bassey's title song was a major hit. Fleming's story was followed closely, except that Blofeld, intent on using the diamonds for a laser attack on Cape

Canaveral, is substituted for the American mafiosi. The screenwriter, Tom Mankiewicz, introduced a girl being thrown from a top window of the casino hotel, only to land in the pool.

Not just one but several Blofelds appear, with white cats, causing Bond to kill the wrong one. The victims include a villainous dentist, killed with a scorpion, and an old lady courier, drowned in an Amsterdam canal. Just when Bond appears to have prevailed, he and the hard boiled Tiffany (Jill St John) have to dispose of two killers attacking them in their suite on the *Queen Elizabeth* (on which Ian Fleming had been a regular traveller).

The film got mainly positive reviews at the time, with good performances by Connery and St John. Since then, it has been rated lower in the list of Bond films. It is difficult to see why, given some later dross. It was extremely popular where it mattered, which was with the 'cheerful reactions' of its audiences.

In 1973, a film at last was made of Fleming's early novel *Live and Let Die*. The new Bond was one of Fleming's original choices, Roger Moore, whose portrayal of Fleming's hero was compared unfavourably by critics to that of Sean Connery. For, beneath the suave exterior, the underlying hint of menace and 'fists at the ready, concealed thuggishness' in Connery's version of Bond was felt to be entirely missing in the 'good looking and likeable', relaxed and self-deprecating Moore. They conceded his charm but observed that, in most situations, his deadliest weapons were likely to be 'a sardonic quip and a raised eyebrow'.

The films with Sean Connery had made small attempts at humour. But they were a long way from playing Bond for laughs, as Moore was required to do in *Live and Let Die* when he escapes by walking over the backs of crocodiles. Mankiewicz vulgarised Fleming's story about Mr Big and Solitaire by introducing a completely alien element in the comical southern Sheriff Pepper, trying in vain to stop the spectacular speedboat chases across the Louisiana bayous. The critical reception was dire, but audiences liked the new sense of humour, with the film earning a record $162 million.

Ian Fleming's next novel, *The Spy Who Loved Me*, was an utter fiasco. In a completely different approach, intended apparently to counter the charges of excessive machismo, it is the account by a young Canadian woman of a series of bad experiences she suffers with men. Bond does not appear until two thirds of the way through. While working at a motel with a dubious owner, she is attacked by two gangsters who plan to burn it down to collect the insurance. They intend to kill her and make it look as if she started the blaze. As she is about to be raped by them, the door buzzer sounds, as Bond has suffered a flat tyre. One of the gangsters has all metal teeth – the model for 'Jaws'.

Bond kills them, makes love to the girl and calls the police. The police captain warns the girl that all men of violence are to be avoided, but she has fallen for the spy who saved her. In an embarrassing passage about Bond's lovemaking skills, Fleming attributes to the girl the view that 'all women love semi-rape. They long to be taken.'

Fleming himself felt that his 'experiment' had gone 'very much awry.' The book got a dire reception, with the *Telegraph* writing, 'Oh dear, oh dear.' Others found it dreary and boring – the dreadest of words to Ian Fleming. Some of the sex scenes got it banned in various countries. *The Times* noted that Bond was less a person than a cult, which deserved better than this. Ian Fleming banned any reprints, cancelled the planned paperback edition and forbade any film ever being made of his book.

And none was. Instead, ironically, in 1977 Ian Fleming's title was attached to one of the best films of the entire Bond series and easily the best of the Roger Moore era, with an entirely new and far better story written by Richard Maibaum and Christopher Wood.

As a British and a Soviet nuclear submarine both have disappeared, Bond has to team up with the KGB agent Anya (Barbara Bach), whose fiancé has been killed by Bond. The film starts with the best prelude of all Bond films: a spectacular breakneck firefight on skis, ending with Bond jumping off a cliff, only to be saved by his Union Jack parachute. This had the premiere audience, including the then Prince Charles, on their feet before the movie had even properly started.

Anya agrees to cooperate with Bond in the mission, but vows to kill him as soon as it is over. Amidst the temples of Luxor, they encounter a formidable new adversary: 'Jaws' (Richard Kiel). Bond tries to kill Jaws by dropping him in a shark tank, but he escapes by attacking a shark. Having prevailed against SPECTRE and Jaws, Anya is about to shoot Bond, but instead they embrace. When 'M' asks what on earth they are doing, Roger Moore replies, 'Keeping the British end up, sir.'

The film was a huge commercial success, with $185 million in takings. One critic found it so spectacular, with so gorgeous an actress and so full of gadgets that, in terms of the improbable plot, it 'deserved to get away with anything'. Most of the others agreed.

The Fleming novel *Moonraker* was filmed hastily in 1979 to take advantage of the huge success of *Star Wars*. Featuring the theft of a space shuttle, it was transformed into a sci-fi thriller that owed almost nothing to Fleming's story. It did, however, contain a favourite Roger Moore Bond scene. When 'M' asks when Bond will return from his trip to Africa, Moneypenny says, 'He's on his last leg, sir.' Cut to Bond on a private jet, caressing a stewardess's thigh. 'Any higher, Mr Bond,' she says, 'and my ears will pop.'

The by now seriously ailing Ian Fleming had told his friend William Plomer that *The Man with the Golden Gun*, published posthumously in 1965, would be his last Bond novel, as he had 'run out of puff and zest'. He had been able to work on the book for only an hour a day and had no chance to revise it. It received rather sad reviews, as not being fully finished and way below Fleming at his best.

It did, however, contain a trademark Fleming ending. Bond is instructed to kill the world's most dangerous contract killer, Scaramanga, who has killed British agents. Wounded and cornered, Scaramanga exploits Bond's Britishness by telling him that he cannot kill a man in cold blood and claims anyway the right to say a final prayer. He then shoots Bond with a tiny gun hidden in the palm of his hand, before being shot and killed.

The 1974 film version had attractive locations but suffered from the completely superfluous reintroduction of the hapless Sheriff Pepper. Ian Fleming's friend, Christopher Lee, delivered a strong performance as Scaramanga. Several scenes were stolen by Britt Ekland as Miss Goodnight. She was denounced by the critics for her scattiness, as all other Bond females had been tough and resourceful as well as gorgeous, and so was Goodnight in Fleming's novel, unlike in the film. But, as one dissenter observed, 'Who cares, as long as she's using her perfect bikini bottom to muck things up.' Britt Ekland ever since has ranked as one of the favourite Bond girls.

One of the less popular Bond movies, there was concern that the takings reached 'only' $97 million. A critic for *The Guardian* contended, as several had before, that Ian Fleming and Bond had 'outlived the spirit of the times'. How could he be expected to know that he was at least fifty years too early in reaching that conclusion?

After a striking start with Shirley Bassey in *Goldfinger*, from 1977 the Bond films carried their very own hit theme songs from a host of well known pop stars, including Madonna, Tina Turner, Tom Jones, Paul McCartney and Adele.

The 1981 film *For Your Eyes Only* earned fame before it appeared, as the striking poster of a girl's legs and rear was thought too adventurous by some US newspapers, who insisted on adding a pair of shorts. The film was partly based on two Fleming short stories, the first about Bond, on an assignment, encountering a vengeful daughter armed with a crossbow, who insists on killing the target herself; the second, entitled 'Risico' (risky), about a flood of heroin into the UK, funded by the Russians.

With Carole Bouquet as the vengeful daughter, it had plenty of action scenes, causing one critic to lament that 'nothing succeeds like excess', which proved to be the case, as it earned nearly $200 million.

The year 1983 was a vintage one for Bond fans, as they faced a choice between Roger Moore and Maud Adams in June in *Octopussy* and Sean Connery and Kim Basinger later in the year in *Never Say Never Again*. Most chose to watch both.

The more 'official' *Octopussy* was produced by Metro-Goldwyn-Mayer with Eon Productions, which had been responsible for the other Bond films (apart from the spoof version of *Casino Royale*). Except for the title and the pursuit of a Fabergé egg, which was based on one of his stories, it had no other contribution from Ian Fleming. It was damned by the critics for the lack of much of a plot.

But with George Macdonald Fraser as part author of the screenplay and memorable locations, especially the lake palace in Udaipur, and plenty of action, it was another of the 'easy to watch' Bond films that proved popular with audiences. It was the first Bond film to be officially released in the Soviet Union, with a gala premiere in Moscow.

Meanwhile, settlement of the long standing legal dispute over *Thunderball* had enabled Ian Fleming's co-writers on that story, Kevin McClory and Jack Whittingham, with a different producer, to convince Sean Connery, after twelve years, to abandon his vow never to play Bond again and to appear with Kim Basinger in a new version, entitled, in Connery's honour, *Never Say Never Again*. It contained some entertaining dialogue between Bond and the *femme fatale*, Fatima Blush, a character worthy of being created by Fleming, who wants Bond to certify that she has been his No. 1 sexual partner, before shooting him:

'Write: "The greatest rapture of my life was in the arms of Fatima Blush."'

'I just remembered. The service won't let me give endorsements.'

Bond then shoots her with a fountain pen.

Connery won easily with the critics. But *Octopussy*, another of the Bond films loved by audiences regardless of the reviews, earned nearly $200 million; *Never Say Never Again* also was successful, though not by quite as much.

The last Roger Moore Bond film, *A View to a Kill*, was one of the weakest of the series, redeemed only by Grace Jones as, initially, the villainess. The first and best phase of the 1987 film, *The Living Daylights*, was based on Fleming's story about the KGB defector, Kostov. The Soviets have found out where and roughly when he plans to cross into West Berlin and have assigned their top sniper, 'Trigger', to kill him.

Surveying the scene, Bond sees an exceptionally beautiful girl carrying a cello case (like Fleming's half-sister, Amaryllis) entering the building opposite. He realises that this must be 'Trigger'. When Kostov makes his run, Bond shoots at her gun, instead of killing the girl. But Kostov turns out to be a fake defector. Timothy Dalton won praise from the critics for portraying a darker, more earnest Bond, though less so from audiences used to the more humorous Roger Moore. Yet the film earned another fortune.

Though Ian Fleming's work did not feature in the subsequent Bond films, except for Daniel Craig's *Casino Royale*, they too all carried his name first on the list of credits for having created and defined the indispensable, iconic figure who remained the principal pole of attraction of the entire series. However varied the locations and extravagant the plots and however many reviewers deplored his character, the absolute imperative was that the 'misogynist dinosaur' (according to Judi Dench, as 'M') must remain fully recognisable as Bond.

The films, even the less memorable ones, vindicated Fleming's belief that those watching them would be happy to follow the story, however far-fetched, if they found Bond, the maidens and the villains sufficiently engaging and were kept wanting to know what happened next. His stories, from the outset, had been envisaged to be filmed, providing the vital, hoped for extra glamour from being able to see, rather than just read about, the gorgeous girls, action scenes and locations he could bring to mind.

One of the most vivid of Bond's stories, *The Hildebrand Rarity*, was one of the few not written with filming in mind. Bond is on a yacht searching for the incredibly rare Hildebrand variety of fish. The brutal owner has an attractive wife, who he beats with a stingray tail. They find the fish, but the yacht's owner pours poison into the water and kills the only one they can find. Having drunk too much, he falls asleep with his mouth open. In the morning he is dead, killed by someone, Bond believes the wife, who has inserted the spiny Rarity, that cannot be coughed out, in his open jaw. Bond tips the corpse into the water, to make it look like an accident, but decides to decline the offer of a cruise with her.

By 1995, Pierce Brosnan had taken over as Bond, receiving generally positive reviews despite having to figure in three of the worst rated Bond movies. His first and best Bond film, *GoldenEye*, had a redoubtable adversary in Xenia Onatopp, who enjoyed asphyxiating men between her thighs, with Famke Janssen's performance in the part earning her a place in the top ten Bond girls. The others were profitable but unmemorable. Those writing the scripts of these movies were running out of imagination.

After these rather tired efforts, in 2006, the Daniel Craig era as Bond opened with a resounding bang with *Casino Royale*, showing the power of an enhanced version of a good Fleming story, a first rate, new, harder edged Bond, with a renewed hint of menace and an excellent *femme fatale* in Eva Green as Vesper Lynd. A super fit Daniel Craig emerges from the sea in a pastiche of Ursula Andress doing so in *Dr. No!* The action is moved to Montenegro and Venice; the game is poker, not baccarat. Vesper commits suicide by drowning, but the tragedy is the same.

The critics praised the new Bond for being 'cold and brutal' and the film for its focus on character and plot and not just on action scenes. Immediately hailed as one of the greatest Bond films, aided by inflation, the film earned over $600 million, four times the also rapidly increasing costs of production.

The 2008 film *Quantum of Solace* paled in comparison with *Casino Royale*. The choice of title was bizarre, as Fleming's short story of that name, written amidst his own domestic problems, was the tale of a marriage in which the 'quantum of solace' between husband and wife falls to zero, which had nothing to do with the film's complicated plot.

The next Craig as Bond film, *Skyfall*, with a brand new plot, the most magnetic of villains in Javier Bardem as the rogue MI6 agent Silva, and Sam Mendes as director, instantly was recognised as right at the top of the Bond movie hierarchy. The song by Adele was a major hit. The story of an ex-MI6 agent abandoned to the Chinese by 'M' was worked on by three scriptwriters then revised by Mendes. The cyberterrorist Silva, disfigured by the cyanide pill he took when handed over to the Chinese, wants revenge on 'M' (Judi Dench) and MI6. Bond drives with her to *Skyfall*, his estate in Scotland, to prepare for battle with his gamekeeper (Albert Finney). 'M' and Silva both are killed.

The premiere was attended by the then Prince Charles and the Duchess of Cornwall. Several critics wondered if *Skyfall* was not the best Bond film ever, with serious characterisation plus lots of action and Sam Mendes, Daniel Craig, Javier Bardem and Albert Finney all getting enthusiastic reviews. The film earned over one billion dollars. (Astonishingly, once adjusted for inflation, this was not much more than the 1965 film *Thunderball*).

The 2015 film, *Spectre*, could hardly fail to be a comedown after *Skyfall*. But it featured a hypnotic performance by Monica Bellucci as a SPECTRE cum mafia widow, eclipsing Léa Seydoux as the psychiatrist Madeleine Swann and introducing Bond viewers to an entirely new experience – a drop dead gorgeous female in her fifties! Dramatic action scenes culminated in the destruction of the MI6 headquarters on the Thames and Blofeld's helicopter being shot down on Westminster Bridge. It earned nearly $900 million, though with sky high production and promotion costs.

In the culminating 2021 film *No Time to Die*, Swann persuades Bond to visit Vesper's grave, where he survives a SPECTRE assassination attempt. Blofeld by now is locked up in Belmarsh prison but is still running SPECTRE while pretending to be insane. An excellent cameo features Ana de Armas as a kickboxing CIA agent, Paloma. The villains are first Blofeld and SPECTRE, then Safin (Rami Malek), who acquire a deadly DNA targeting bioweapon.

Blofeld reveals that he arranged the explosion at Vesper's grave to make Bond suspicious of Swann. The nanobots kill Blofeld while Bond is trying to strangle him, but he infects Bond with a DNA programme designed to kill Swann and her child who, hitherto, she has denied is Bond's daughter. But when a now for the first time very vulnerable Bond climbs a ladder to say goodbye to them, Swann says, 'She does have your eyes.'

'I know; I know,' replies Bond.

Bond opens the silo doors to allow the missiles from HMS *Dragon* to destroy the site. He rejects the chance to join Swann and his daughter, Mathilde, as doing so would kill them, so he is killed by his own side's missiles.

Afterwards, Swann starts telling her child a story about a man named 'Bond, James Bond...'

Toasting Bond's memory with Moneypenny and Q, 'M' recites both Ian Fleming's and Bond's favourite lines from Jack London:

'The proper function of man is to live, not to exist. I shall not waste my days in trying to prolong them.'

Although not admired as much as *Skyfall*, excruciatingly long and with an over complicated plot, *No Time to Die* got an enthusiastic reception as a fitting end and climax to Daniel Craig's career as Bond, with excellent reviews in the British and American press. Associated Press declared that 'Bond and Fleming were fun... Life will be less interesting without them.' Ian Fleming was credited by the BBC with having created 'the ultimate escapist hero ... the most stupendous set pieces, the sensuous phrases.' Others noted that he had sought to portray Bond as the 'epitome of Englishness'. Barbara Broccoli, who succeeded her father in charge of the film franchise, felt that Ian Fleming's creation owed much to his experience amidst the 'heroism' of Britain in the Second World War.

Time magazine hailed Daniel Craig as the best of Bonds but was sceptical that there was any longer a place for Bond in the world of 'Me Too', accusing Bond not only of 'bearing ill feelings towards women' (rather than liking them too much), but of rape, of which there was zero evidence in any Bond film or Fleming novel. This extraordinary review was interesting as revealing a fundamental misunderstanding of the Bond franchise.

For *Time* apparently were unaware that no Bond film was ever permitted to be produced without a PG13 rating, enabling it to be seen by all teenagers and adults, frequently at the same time, creating an especially attractive entertainment for families, who were the target audience for Bond films. All of them were self-censored before they were released. No steamy scene was allowed to be shown in any Bond film. Unless they were villainesses trying to kill him, like Onatopp, none of the feisty and independent heroines of these movies, when they fell into his arms, were permitted to receive anything more from Bond than a hug. In a sign of the times, however, in 2023 Ian Fleming Publications announced a very mild sanitisation of his novels on the lines of the changes Ian Fleming himself had made for the US edition of *Live and Let Die*.

Some of the critics might, perhaps, be forgiven for hoping that, for them, the agony is over of having to review Bond films that, however run of the mill they were and however dismissive they were about them, still found audiences flocking to see them and, *in every case*, were a commercial success. Roger Moore and the writer Richard Maibaum never got as much credit as they deserved for the first successful reboot of the series towards a more humorous version of Bond. What kept worldwide audiences flocking to the films was the expectation of having fun, of participating in their *manifest joie de vivre*. The second successful reboot, by Daniel Craig, was badly needed too, as no one should want to see so extraordinary a saga die an ignoble death by becoming boring.

The Bond films to date have earned seven billion dollars worldwide, including two billion from the United States. MGM confirmed that, despite its vast expense, *No Time to Die* was profitable. But blockbuster films like it and *Spectre*, with more and more complicated stories and ever more spectacular cinematography and stunts, entailed ever increasing costs of production and promotion.

In July 2012, Bond had received a definitive royal blessing when a veteran fan, Queen Elizabeth, with her corgis, greeted Daniel Craig at Buckingham Palace with, 'Good evening, Mr. Bond.' There followed a pretend parachute jump by Craig and the Queen into the Millennium Stadium for the opening of the London Summer Olympic Games. Showing a shrewd appreciation of the different

Bond personas, the Queen teased Craig before the photographers with, 'He is the one who doesn't smile!'

At the end of the credits for *No Time to Die*, there is a declaration that 'James Bond will return', giving Bond devotees worldwide hopes and a belief that a way will be found to enable him to rise from the ashes, as Barbara Broccoli seems determined to do. She has declared that any future Bond will be male, in accordance with the iconic image. Despite his apparently definitive disappearance on this occasion, there remain infinite possibilities for his return. We all would like to know, for instance, how it was that Bond earned his licence to kill.

CHAPTER XIX

JOHN LE CARRÉ

David Cornwell, who became John le Carré, was born in Poole, Dorset in 1931. He had an extraordinary family history that had a profound effect on him. For his mother abandoned his roguish, confidence trickster father, Ronnie, and their children when he was five. He had run through all her money and had been jailed for fraud. She left with someone she later married called John Hill.

When David was twenty-one, he wrote a letter to his mother, leading to a meeting with her. She told him that his father had infected her with syphilis but had no explanation for simply abandoning the boys. She in turn was left by her new husband in Canada. When she returned to Britain, David, by now le Carré, bought for her a house in Suffolk. Periodically, he visited her and later paid for her nursing home fees and arranged her funeral.

Throughout David Cornwell's childhood, the family had severe financial problems. He recalled having been beaten by his father (though not with much conviction), but had a complex relationship with him, as his father could be charismatic as well as deceitful. In his novel *A Perfect Spy*, Rick Pym, a scheming swindler and father of the protagonist, Magnus Pym, was based on le Carré's father, Ronnie. His father had a series of girlfriends before marrying an attractive young woman, Jean Gronow, in 1944. David became fond of her.

Ronnie could be very convincing. Periodically, some of his always risky speculative ventures would come off, making him for a while very rich, though still living on the edge of the law. With, in his more fortunate times, an office in Mayfair and a Bentley with a personalised number plate, Ronnie was spending money as fast as he made it. Partly because David's elder brother, Tony, was a promising cricketer, later playing for Dorset, in 1948 he gave a party for the visiting Australian cricket team.

David was educated at a public school, Sherborne, where he did well but which he actively disliked. He left a year early to escape from his father and spend a year studying languages at the University of Bern. As cheques from his father bounced, he found casual work to survive. While there, he was approached by a lady from the British Consulate, who asked him to report on left wing student groups and British students involved in them, which he agreed to do. In St Moritz, he met his future wife, Ann Sharp.

In 1950, he was called up for national service and served as an Army Intelligence Corps officer in the garrison in Allied occupied Austria, interrogating German speakers who had crossed into the West.

He then was admitted to Lincoln College, Oxford, where, thanks to some much better off friends, he joined the Gridiron Club. This was not long after the defection of Burgess and Maclean, causing MI5 to conclude that it needed to know more about communist sympathisers in the universities. David was recruited by MI5 to report covertly on left wing student groups who might be susceptible to Soviet influence. He joined both the Communist and Socialist Clubs and attended meetings of the Anglo-Soviet Friendship Society.

Unpleasant as it was to be informing on his supposed friends, David did not find it disgraceful, his later argument (once he had become John le Carré) being that someone had to do it.

At Lincoln College, David had found an important mentor in the senior tutor Vivian Green, supposedly one of the future models for his hero Smiley. As Ronnie by now was facing bankruptcy, MI5 considered taking on David full time to infiltrate far left student circles. The idea was vetoed by Dick White, head of MI5, who did not like the idea of using someone so young as a double agent.

David wanted to get married and be free of his father. So he had to leave Oxford at the end of his second year to take a teaching job for a year at a school in Somerset. He was twenty-three; his wife, Ann, was twenty-two. He then returned to Lincoln College to graduate with first class honours in modern languages. Thereafter, he taught French and German at Eton for two years.

He proved to be good at teaching there but claimed that any teacher at Eton lived midway between the high table and the servants' quarters. He disliked the arrogance and sense of entitlement of some of the pupils there, especially among the stupider boys, and their feeling that they were part of a *Herrenvolk*. Asked about his time at Eton years later, he said that 'those who knock the upper classes have no idea how dreadful they are' and claimed that it gave him a 'unique insight into the criminal mind'!

David had been educated entirely at private schools. But his very difficult upbringing had left him with huge resentment towards those who, by birth, had been more fortunate than him, though he did not find it difficult to compete with them and counted quite a few friends among them. It was difficult to find much evidence of actual damage he suffered from the 'toffs' he despised, but the resentment was real.

In politics, he blamed what he regarded as the huge mistakes by David Cameron and Boris Johnson resulting in Britain's exit from the European Union as based on the sense of entitlement and overweening over-confidence that, in his view, had been inculcated in them at Eton.

It was while at Eton that, in 1958, he decided to become a full time member of MI5. He worked on his first novel, *Call for the Dead*, while commuting by train to the MI5 headquarters in Mayfair. He ran agents, conducted interrogations and arranged the tapping of suspects' phones. His mentor there was John Bingham, later Lord Clanmorris, who wrote crime novels himself. He was very impressed by the care Bingham took in protecting his agents, making him, with Vivian Green, part of the model for the future Smiley.

In theory, he should have felt at home in MI5, doing counter espionage work that he accepted was necessary amidst a down to earth workforce. Many of his colleagues there disliked the far more highfalutin MI6 (sometimes referred to as 'those shits across the park'), who claimed to be better bred and still believed that Philby was innocent. But David was unimpressed by what he regarded as the prevailing mediocrity in MI5, especially those who were former police officers from the colonies.

So, in 1960, the future John le Carré applied to join the more glamorous MI6, which offered the attraction of spying overseas, as against counter spying at home. He was despatched as, ostensibly, an ordinary Second Secretary in the Foreign Service to the British Embassy in Bonn. That he worked for MI6 was not disclosed to the German authorities.

For the next twenty years, David refused to admit that he had been a spy, though the success of his books, with their apparent realism, was helped by the supposition that he had been one. His role was to report on the right wing groups and organisations who, it was feared, might stage a comeback in Germany. This must have entailed spending a lot of time in beer halls. It must also have been excruciatingly boring, as the feared right wing revival never looked like taking place. On a couple of occasions, he interpreted for a forlorn Harold Macmillan pleading, unsuccessfully, for Britain to be allowed to join the European Economic Community.

David knew that John Bingham had been able to publish novels while a member of MI5. When *Call for the Dead* was accepted for publication by Victor Gollancz, David submitted it for clearance to MI6, who required only one minor change but stipulated that it must be published under a pseudonym. He chose John le Carré, for reasons he claimed later to be unable to recall.

The depiction of espionage that he was aiming for in his books was one of gritty realism, the antithesis of the glamorous universe of James Bond, who he regarded as not a spy, but 'an international gangster'. He deplored the success of the Bond films, which he considered vulgar. So, he set about creating a no less iconic figure of his own.

Call for the Dead introduced the apparently ordinary, in reality extraordinary, George Smiley, a member of the 'Circus' controlling

British intelligence. Smiley is depicted as an out of shape, middle aged bureaucrat, with a serially unfaithful wife. The name, 'Circus,' was derived from Cambridge Circus, which David portrayed as the venue for MI6 headquarters, rather than the real HQ at Broadway, by St James's Park. It also reflected the manner in which le Carré believed it at times to be capable of acting.

Looking into the apparent suicide of a Foreign Office official, Smiley discovers that he and, especially, his wife had been passing secrets to an East German agent, Hans-Dieter Mundt, who reappears as head of the East German secret service in le Carré's third novel, *The Spy Who Came in from the Cold*. His second novel, *A Murder of Quality*, was simply a murder mystery that Smiley helped to solve.

His very obvious talent as a writer had ensured that his first two books were well reviewed. In 1963, he shot out the lights with his breakthrough novel, *The Spy Who Came in from the Cold*. This was the story of Alec Leamas, a British secret agent being sent to East Germany as a false defector. Leamas wants to leave the service and 'come in from the cold', as his last agent in East Germany has been killed. Instead, to support his defector story, he has to plunge into heavy drinking, pretend to have stolen money and go to prison for assault. While living in poverty, he falls in love with a young communist, Liz Gold. On leaving for East Germany, he asks Smiley to leave Liz alone.

The objective is for Leamas to incriminate Mundt, now head of East German counter-intelligence, as a British agent, as Mundt's deputy, Fiedler, has become suspicious of him. But Liz appears, having been invited by the East Germans. In their court hearing, she reveals that Smiley had paid her rent arrears, blowing Leamas's cover. The thuggish Mundt, who has in fact become a British agent, uses this to discredit the more idealistic Fiedler. Leamas and Liz are taken to the Berlin Wall, but Liz is shot as they try to climb over. As Smiley calls to him to cross, a disillusioned Lemas goes back to help Liz and be killed with her, thereby coming in from the cold.

So the 'Circus' had been responsible for a fiendishly clever, heartless plot, which had got its agent and the innocent Liz killed. An award winning film was made of the story, with Richard Burton as Leamas and Claire Bloom as Liz. This very powerful novel got an ecstatic reception from its reviewers and quickly was rated one of the best crime thrillers of all time. It was endorsed by Graham Greene as 'the best spy story I have ever read'.

Christopher Andrew, the foremost historian of the British intelligence services, recorded his astonishment as reviewer after reviewer rated it as amazingly realistic, though it portrayed the British services as acting in just as immoral and murderous a manner as their adversaries. This moral equivalence was emphasised in Leamas's statement to Liz that all spies are 'a squalid procession of vain fools, traitors, too, yes; pansies, sadists and drunkards, people who play cowboys and Indians with other people's lives.'

This did not go down well with David's colleagues in MI6, who considered that nothing in his experience with them could have led him to believe that they would operate in such a way. No wildly improbable plan of the kind he had fabricated would have been considered, let alone implemented, and nor would any of their agents been treated as he described.

Kim Philby, in a letter he wrote to the wife he left behind in Beirut, admired the sophistication of *The Spy Who Came in from the Cold* 'after all that James Bond idiocy,' but had to admit 'that the whole lot, from beginning to end, is basically implausible – at any rate to anyone who has any real knowledge of the business'.

But David's work became the bestselling novel in the US in 1964, making him a celebrity there. As le Carré, then and later, he insisted that his works were pure fiction, but he had intended *The Spy Who Came in from the Cold* to show that espionage as practised by the 'Circus' was just as immoral as that of their adversaries.

As he wrote in a foreword to the Penguin edition of his next novel, he was concerned that, instead, Leamas had been regarded by most British readers as a tragic hero. So, *The Looking Glass War* was intended by him to re-emphasise the immorality of the profession, depicting an incompetent 'Department' sacrificing an over the hill Polish agent, killed in pursuit of a non-existent missile site in East Germany, in an attempt to justify its own existence. It was, he said, an explicit satire about a spy operation that was completely futile and pointless, seeking to counter British nostalgia for the glory days of the Second World War.

He was alarmed at the reaction, as the book got some scathing reviews and his readers 'hated me for it'. The British public proved reluctant to believe that the intelligence agencies were as hopeless as he portrayed them. They still loved their spies. 'No matter how often they trip over their cloaks and leave their daggers on the train to Tonbridge, they do no wrong.' The book was turned into a not very successful film.

David had been transferred to the British Consulate in Hamburg to give him a lower profile in Germany. MI6 and the Foreign Office had cleared *The Looking Glass War*, presumably because they regarded it as self-evidently fictional.

In 1964, he resigned from MI6. He claimed later that his cover had been blown by Philby. This cannot have been the case, as Philby had been in Beirut since before David arrived in Bonn. In reality, David wanted to be free to concentrate on his writing. His identity by this time had been discovered by the press, though he continued to deny any role as a spy.

The by now le Carré later suggested that Dick White had told him that if he stayed in the service, he could rise to the 'top job'. None of his SIS colleagues believed this, as he was so junior and had been with them for so short a time.

When White saw his counterpart in Washington, what he did say was that le Carré 'hasn't done us any good. He makes all intelligence officers look like philanderers and drunks. He's presenting a Service without trust or loyalty, where agents are sacrificed without compunction.' His portrayal of cynicism, defeatism and lack of conviction suggested that the cause was not worthwhile. He was getting his revenge on the 'old school ties' in British intelligence. David's former mentor, John Bingham, also was fed up with his portrayal of bleakness and nihilism in the intelligence service, considering David to have 'fouled his nest after leaving it'.

Richard Helms, head of the CIA, regarded his portrait of British intelligence as a viciously negative portrayal of highly motivated, patriotic officers trying to do their best for their country and its allies in countering the efforts of evil regimes in the Soviet Union and East Germany.

The next le Carré novel, *A Small Town in Germany*, is the story of a Foreign Office official, Turner, investigating the disappearance with a confidential file of a minor official in the British Embassy in Bonn, Harting. Turner discovers that the file is about the Nazi past of a fast rising right wing industrialist, Karfeld. The embassy's head of chancery, Bradfield, wants to cover this up. Harting had tried to shoot Karfeld once and tries and misses again at Karfeld's next rally. Turner watches helplessly as Karfeld's supporters kill Harting and find and destroy the evidence against him.

The book got mixed reviews. It made it onto the bestseller list in America, but no film was made of it (though a BBC TV series was) and the reception fell far short of that for *The Spy Who Came in from the Cold*.

In what had become a familiar pattern, the le Carré portrayal of the dismal part played by the Bonn Embassy in this drama infuriated some of his former colleagues. The embassy at the time included Tony Duff who, though not a spy, became head of MI5, Julian Bullard, who became an outstanding British Ambassador there and David Cornwell's friend, David Goodall, who later played a vital role in the negotiations to end the conflict in Northern Ireland. Goodall and David's other Foreign Service friend, John Margetson, grew tired of explaining to their colleagues that it was essential to le Carré's fiction to portray British diplomats as nincompoops, or worse.

As Kim Philby was about to publish his memoir, David as le Carré was asked to write an article, which became the introduction to a book about him. In it, he sought to portray Philby as a kindred spirit, equally outraged by the British establishment and kindred also in their attitude to women.

His article was made fun of, among others, by Graham Greene, who pointed out that the word 'establishment' was used seventeen times in fifteen pages. David had missed the whole point about Philby, which was that he was not like David's soul searching self at all, or David's future traitor Bill Haydon, but a *true believer ideological spy*, convinced that he was serving a higher cause.

By this time, David had discovered a 'soulmate', as he believed, in the charismatic young author of a successful novel, made into a film, *Tunes of Glory*. James Kennaway was a far wilder character than David. He had an attractive wife, Susan, but spent a holiday with David in Paris with the two of them, especially James, carousing with girls, mainly prostitutes. This seemed wonderful to David, extremely restive in his marriage. Watching the classic movie of a threesome, *Jules et Jim*, Susan held hands with both of them.

Before long, David had embarked on an affair with her. When her husband found out, huge scenes followed, but David told her that he did not have the guts to inflict more pain on his wife. He never saw Kennaway again; he died from a heart attack aged only forty. From that point on, David pursued other women as enthusiastically as his former friend had done. Meanwhile, he received fervent appeals from his father in various parts of the world, all of them asking for money, plus some for help in getting him out of jail.

In 1970, David wrote to Ann from Malibu, 'I think we should dissolve our marriage.' When they divorced, he married Jane Eustace, who had worked for his publishers, Hodder and Stoughton. It was quite a civilised divorce, as Ann soon remarried too. David continued to try to be a good father to his children; he also helped his half-sister, Charlotte. But, according to David, it was made clear to Jane from the outset that 'there will be other women'.

His next novel, *The Naïve and Sentimental Lover*, was based on his triangular relationship with the Kennaways. The book got a dire reception, with publishers and critics alike urging David to go back to his genre, which was spy fiction. He reacted rather bitterly but took their advice. The result was David embarking on what most of his admirers regarded as his very best work. Inspired by the enduring interest in Kim Philby, this was the trilogy describing Smiley's struggle against his Soviet counterpart, 'Karla', beginning with, for many, their favourite of all le Carré's novels, *Tinker Tailor Soldier Spy*.

Smiley has been sacked for suggesting that there is a high level 'mole' in the Circus. Now, he is recalled to investigate. The novel provides a realistic description of the working environment and warren of tunnels in the old MI6 headquarters in Broadway. The mole, code named 'Gerald', is hiding in plain sight, as the most prized intelligence in the Circus is coming from a Russian agent, Polyakov, who in turn is fed supposedly harmless information to pass to the other side.

Jim Prideaux, now retired, was sent to meet a supposed defector in Czechoslovakia, only to be shot and interrogated by Karla. (It is difficult for the reader to understand why he went into so obvious an ambush.) The fiasco caused the former Control to be replaced and Smiley sidelined, Karla's objective being to protect the 'mole'. This can only be one of the most senior people in the Circus, with Smiley sifting through the suspects.

Smiley is convinced that Polyakov is controlled by Karla and the real flow of information is to and not from him. One of the suspects, Bill Haydon, is having an affair with Smiley's unfaithful wife, as instructed by Karla, so that Smiley might fear that he was suspecting Haydon for the wrong, rather than the right, reasons. But Smiley traps Haydon, who confesses. While waiting to be traded for Soviet prisoners, Haydon is shot by an unidentified assassin, who Smiley realises is Prideaux, with whom Haydon had a homosexual affair in their youth.

Amidst all the le Carré novels, this was a true masterpiece, with full development of the magnetic character of Smiley, the pudgy and cuckolded but supremely intelligent antithesis of James Bond. It got the enthusiastic reception it deserved, as an apparently very realistic portrait of the internal workings and machinations of an intelligence organisation and first class characterisations of the figures within it. Published first in America, as David felt that he got a better reception there, the book became No. 1 in the bestseller lists in both Britain and America. It is hard to think of any better spy novel.

In the BBC television series based on this and the other Smiley novels, Alec Guinness delivered an unforgettable performance as Smiley. The series ever since has been rated as one of the very best of all BBC television productions. This was followed in 2011 by a successful film, with Gary Oldman as Smiley and Colin Firth as Haydon.

The one serious weakness in this story was Haydon's explanation for becoming a traitor. Instead of revealing that he did so as a committed communist, which he wasn't, or did it for money, which he didn't, he explains that he hated the Americans but then spied against Britain too, because of the country's declining position in the world following the Suez fiasco (a perennial le Carré theme). Le Carré was strongly anti-American too.

In 1975, David's father died suddenly, with all his assets mortgaged to the hilt and tax claims against him. David attended his cremation but not his memorial service. Far from regretting him, David professed privately to have felt liberated by his father's death.

To conduct research for his next novel, David headed for Hong Kong, then for Indo-China, with an expert on the region, David Greenway. After they travelled together, David kept exaggerating the dangers they had faced, telling Greenway, whenever he protested, 'I am a novelist.'

The Honourable Schoolboy, the second book in the Karla trilogy, though a worthy follow up, was not as apparently realistic as the first. Smiley discovers that a senior Chinese official, Nelson, brother of the drug lord Drake Ko, is a Soviet agent. Smiley plans to use this knowledge to turn him into a British agent. The plan is shared with the American 'cousins', who agree that this should be a British operation but with a time limit, following which they will arrest Drake Ko for drug dealing.

But the main concern of the British part time agent and journalist Westerby becomes to rescue Drake Ko's mistress, Lizzie. To do so, he tries to warn Drake of Smiley's plan. When Nelson Ko lands on a remote shore in Hong Kong, CIA forces seize him, leaving the outcome an American success, not that of Smiley. This had secretly been agreed, without Smiley's knowledge, by the British government representative (whatever information was extracted from Nelson would be shared with the Brits anyway).

Smiley, once again, is retired, only to bounce back in the final volume of the trilogy, *Smiley's People*. Smiley discovers that Karla has diverted secret funds to keep his troubled daughter in a mental institution in Switzerland, where she claims to have a powerful father 'who can make people disappear'. When Karla in the end agrees to defect, he throws down in front of Smiley the cigarette lighter, a present from his errant wife, which Karla had pocketed at their previous meeting in a New Delhi jail. Smiley chooses not to pick it up.

At Christmas 1982, Alasdair Milne, Director General of the BBC, sent Margaret Thatcher the tapes of *Yes, Minister* and those of Alec Guinness in the Karla trilogy for her and Denis Thatcher to watch at Chequers, getting a reply from her that 'we tackled the Smiley's three at a time and then two *Yes, Ministers*. All are superb.'

When a friend of his told the Prime Minister that le Carré thought she was very sexy, her reply was, 'No, I am not.' When he was unable to attend a literary dinner with Margaret Thatcher as Prime Minister, he wrote to say, 'Please give her my good wishes. I never thought I could find her admirable, but I do. Even though the immediate consequences, at least, are so wretched. Perhaps because I really do believe that she is an honest and extraordinarily brave person.'

He later refused a CBE from her and a knighthood from her successors. But perhaps he understood that she too did not have a lot of time for the old 'establishment' and her ambition to arrest and reverse Britain's decline in the world, which he kept advertising.

A Perfect Spy, published in 1986, is le Carré's semi-autobiographical story of the British agent, then double agent, Magnus Pym, with a superb portrayal of his relationship with his charismatic conman and alter ego father Rick. It was, le Carré declared, the novel 'a very shrewd psychiatrist' would have encouraged him to write. It was hailed by Philip Roth as 'the best English novel since the war'. (Better than George Orwell, or Graham Greene?) But, grasping the attention of the reader through all its nearly five hundred pages, amidst all twenty-seven of his novels, it is le Carré's hypnotising, other masterpiece.

Magnus is recruited at Oxford by the British and from Bern by the Czechs. There are memorable characterisations of his wife, who realises that he isn't quite what he seems, his straightforward British spymaster, Jack, and his much subtler Czech guru, Axel. The Americans have become suspicious, but his British colleagues defend him, as they did Philby. When he disappears, Jack worries about saving all his Czech agents, but he doesn't need to, as they have all been working for the other side.

Magnus explains to himself that if the British hadn't recruited him to spy, the Czechs wouldn't have done so either. Having finally run out of rope, to the dismay of Axel (and, he must have foreseen, relief of the British), instead of defecting, le Carré's hero/anti hero takes the honourable way out, by shooting himself. Like his father, he had charmed and deceived everyone, including his wife and son, making him the perfect spy.

A perceptive reviewer noted the Dickensian qualities of le Carré's fiction, 'with one big difference'. Dickens, unlike the far bleaker le Carré, 'loved the world and, in his fiction and his life, believed that much could be done to make it a better place.'

As the Cold War drew to an end, le Carré considered that it 'afforded no victory and fighting it no virtue', which was far from being the opinion of the people of eastern Europe. On his behalf, Smiley observed that 'the right side lost, but the wrong side won'. Having defeated communism, how, le Carré worried, was it now going to be possible to defeat the excesses of capitalism?

He conducted extensive research for one of the best of his post Cold War novels, *The Little Drummer Girl*, published in 1983. This was the story of a left wing English actress, Charlie, who thought she was supporting the Palestinian cause only to find that she had been used by Mossad to track down and kill a Palestinian terrorist, Khalil.

While researching it, le Carré met a former head of Israeli intelligence. When, after immense difficulties, he managed also to meet Yasser Arafat in a half destroyed building in Beirut, he said that he had come to 'put his hand on the Palestinian heart'. Pressing le Carré's hand to his chest, 'It is here, it is here,' said Arafat.

Le Carré attacked the Israeli invasion of Lebanon and wanted to see more sympathy shown for the Palestinian cause. But, displaying far greater objectivity than in most of his later novels, he understood the Israeli dilemma and the drama of two peoples with claims to the same territory. His book was attacked as antisemitic by a number of Jewish critics and pro-Israel supporters, but the moderate President of Israel, Chaim Herzog, described it as realistic. William Buckley considered it to be far more than a mere spy story, praising it for 'transcending the genre'. Attracting massive publicity, it was a major success, though not as a film, in which Diane Keaton was miscast as Charlie.

The Russia House was a well received story, turned into a successful film, with Sean Connery handing over all the CIA's questions about Russian nuclear capabilities to secure the release of his girlfriend Katya (played, with an impressive Russian accent, by Michelle Pfeiffer). There followed *The Night Manager*, about the unsuccessful efforts of a former British soldier to bring down 'the most evil man in the world', an international arms dealer, who (of course) has connections in the Western intelligence services.

He then tried his hand at satire in *The Tailor of Panama*, an amusing account of entirely pseudo intelligence activities, made into a film with Pierce Brosnan. Le Carré could not, however, help himself turning the ending into a tragedy. The US invades Panama, based on the hero's fantasies. It was a long step down from Graham Greene's *Our Man in Havana*.

Next there came a huge turning point in his fiction, with all his former subtlety and ambiguity gone and the author instead transformed into a passionate polemicist. *The Constant Gardener* was inspired by a case in Kano, Nigeria, in 1966 when Pfizer tested a new meningitis drug on Nigerian children, eleven of whom died.

The novel is about the brutal murder in Kenya of a British diplomat's human rights activist wife, Tessa, who has discovered that an international pharmaceutical company, under the cover of Aids testing, is experimenting with a drug with dangerous side effects. This is covered up by the corrupt Sir Bernard Pellegrin, head of the Africa desk in the British Foreign Office. Tessa's mild mannered husband, Justin, is determined to find out the truth. At the end, Pellegrin conspires with the pharmaceutical company to pretend that Justin has committed suicide from grief; in reality, he too was murdered.

In publicising his book, le Carré declared that the pharmaceutical industry afforded the most eloquent example of 'the crimes of unbridled capitalism'. His journey through 'the pharmaceutical jungle' had made him realise that, in comparison with reality, his account was 'merely a holiday postcard'.

Reviewers found this hard to credit, given that, in his novel, the pharmaceutical company is responsible for organising brutal murders. In a postscript, he was obliged to apologise for suggesting that the British High Commission in Nairobi had colluded in these.

The book was a huge success, becoming a No. 1 bestseller in Britain and Europe. In the equally successful film version, Rachel Weisz won an Oscar for her memorable performance as Tessa.

But not everyone was enthused by le Carré's display of rage. In the *New York Review of Books*, Hilary Mantel described it as 'a polemic cast in the form of a thriller ... a strident, furious, hasty and at times embarrassing book.' This was the point at which le Carré started to lose his hitherto admiring American audience, as other reviewers there were unimpressed by his wild declarations about an industry that, notwithstanding its serious misdeeds, alone was capable of saving the world from Aids and other pandemics. The *New York Times*, usually so complimentary about his work, declared the story a disappointing stereotype.

Others described it as an angry diatribe, the more so as in the year before *The Constant Gardener* was published, President Mbeki of South Africa had launched a similar attack on 'Big Pharma' in Africa, obstructing the uptake in South Africa of Western medicines for Aids.

So the huge success of *The Constant Gardener* turned out to be a pyrrhic victory for le Carré. His response was to say that 'he could never quite accept' the way his book had been received in America. He was 'becoming seriously imbalanced about America altogether'. As if to demonstrate this, his next book, *Absolute Friends*, ended with the two naïve protagonists, who had inadvertently received a consignment of weapons, being killed by US special forces as if they were terrorists, with a British and American cover up thereafter.

This time, the British critics too felt that his tone was becoming 'wearisome'. George Walden considered that 'a once entertaining writer is subsiding into ranting moralism.' The *New York Times* described the book as 'bashing the reader over the head with dubious assertions,' with all reviewers noting his increasingly intense anti-Americanism. He chose to ignore warnings from friends about the dangers of becoming characterised as an unpleasantly sanctimonious 'angry old man, ranting from his Cornish crag'. He already had left behind a trail of discarded agents and publishers. As his sales in the US plummeted, he did so again, though, as Bob Gottlieb pointed out, the fault lay with the author.

Le Carré always had been a Labour supporting man of the left, but his radicalism now was intensified by the US led invasion of Iraq and Tony Blair's role in supporting it. He blamed Blair and 'New Labour' not only for that but for abandoning socialism. He saw the United States as responsible for most of the world's ills and as 'heading straight down the road to institutional racism and neo-fascism'. By 2005, he saw Britain as 'sliding towards fascism' too.

He regarded the West as primarily responsible for Iran's problems and started an ill advised feud with Salman Rushdie by writing, in response to the *fatwa* against him, that 'nobody has a God given right to insult a great religion ... with impunity'. He was horrified by Donald Trump and described Boris Johnson as 'a pig ignorant Foreign Secretary.' He was incandescent about Brexit, which he described as Britain's 'greatest idiocy', causing him to abandon British and take out Irish citizenship.

In writing his excellent biography of his friend John le Carré,

David Sisman found his subject frequently varying the stories he told him. His cover in Germany was not blown by Kim Philby, his critic, Eliza Manningham-Buller, then head of MI5, had no reason to believe that he 'ran one of our most prolific and successful agents' during his two years there, and he did not write *The Spy Who Came in from the Cold* in five weeks as an anguished response to the building of the Berlin Wall, as he claimed. And so forth.

As his biography was on the verge of being released, Sisman was astonished to learn that le Carré intended, shortly thereafter, to publish an account of his own in *The Pigeon Tunnel*, which he planned as 'some sort of antidote' to the already very admiring and circumspect account by Sisman. Sisman ended up feeling obliged to publish a follow up volume, *The Secret Life of John le Carré*, to cover the innumerable affairs that had been such an important aspect of his life.

Le Carré's rationale for these was that they were vital for his creativity as a writer, which may have been true, as they required him to practise almost exactly the same techniques of deception and tradecraft, including codes and safe houses, as those he had learned to employ in the intelligence services. As with Ian Fleming, all his lovers were volunteers; they were happy to enjoy affairs with the famous writer. Mostly, they did not enjoy them for very long, as le Carré tended soon to be looking for an escape and often did so quite brutally. While most of Ian Fleming's girlfriends seemed to think quite fondly of him thereafter, this was not the case with those of le Carré.

In terms of his stature as a writer, it is difficult to think of any spy novels better than le Carré at his very best in *Tinker Tailor Soldier*

Spy and *A Perfect Spy*. A host of commentators were right to conclude that his best works transcended spy novels, for they were serious works of literature, penned by an extraordinary storyteller. As for their supposed realism, he was an absolute master of creating a realistic atmosphere and the characterisation, especially of the male players, within it. Far less realistic were the stories he was telling, with huge improbabilities in virtually every plot, including in *A Perfect Spy*, where Magnus's treachery is attributed to nothing more than a congenital predisposition, plus friendship with a Czech spy.

Although himself a leading member of the literary establishment, his antipathy to it in all other forms led to some tedious caricatures. Foreign Office officials were almost invariably toffee-nosed, awful and frequently corrupt. With the honourable exceptions of Smiley and Guillam, British intelligence agents were no better than their counterparts in the KGB or *Stasi* or the present day poisoners in Russian military intelligence, while their American 'cousins' were simply insufferable.

No credit was given to them for being determined to try to keep their countries a safer place than they would have been without them. There were plenty of smaller scale Smileys among them, entitled to believe that they were serving in an honourable cause. The latter day heads of MI6 decided, sensibly, that it was a waste of time to protest about such travesties and chose instead to invite him to occasional events as, more or less, an honorary member of the intelligence community, while never taking seriously his pretensions to moral superiority. As one of them observed to me, 'Not many of us agreed to spy on our fellow students at Oxford.'

Some enthusiastic reviewers, impressed by his extraordinary literary skill, were carried away enough to suggest that his novels were about the human condition. This could be true only if they took as bleak a view of the world and humanity as le Carré did. The *New York Times* described *The Spy Who Came in from the Cold* as ending in futility. The same could be said of *The Constant Gardener* and so many other of his stories, ending only in defeat for the principal protagonists, with officialdom against them and the world not at all a better place for their efforts.

By virtue of his main subject, and perhaps to some degree of his own complicated nature, the dominant le Carré theme was not the human condition but deception and betrayal, described with exceptional expertise and expressed with increasing bitterness as he looked sanctimoniously down on the, to him, very disappointing world from his eyrie in Cornwall. Le Carré wrote about his own 'great failure to find happiness'. While aiming successfully, from a literary point of view, far higher than Ian Fleming, the other difference between them was the complete absence in le Carré's world of anything approaching Fleming's or Bond's *joie de vivre*.

None of which can detract from le Carré's extraordinary skill as author of at least two of the best ever spy novels or his wonderful creation, Smiley, who actually did resemble one of the British spymasters of the time.

CHAPTER XX

NEXT STOP EXECUTION

There follows a story, that of Oleg Gordievsky, who described unforgettably at the outset of his book *Next Stop Execution* an episode that, in terms of drama, suspense and sheer terror, puts all fictional spy stories to shame. This was the centrepiece also of Ben Macintyre's book *The Spy and the Traitor*.

At the height of the Cold War, it was extremely difficult for the Western intelligence agencies to recruit any worthwhile Soviet agents. Thanks to the covert communist sympathisers in Western agencies, the flow of secret information was towards Moscow, not from it. A first important breakthrough came when, in July 1960, Oleg Penkovsky, a colonel in Soviet military intelligence (the GRU) gave some American students on a bridge in Moscow a package for the US Embassy. Fearing a provocation, the embassy declined to follow up.

Instead, British intelligence recruited a businessman, Greville Wynne, who was a regular visitor to Moscow, to communicate with Penkovsky, who met British and American intelligence officers in

London in April 1961. Over the next eighteen months, he supplied a large number of documents, with specifics about Soviet nuclear capabilities. These included descriptions of the nuclear rocket launch sites being built in Cuba, confirmed by US aerial surveillance.

The revelation by Penkovsky that Soviet nuclear programmes were far less developed than Khrushchev was pretending (or than the CIA had estimated), plus the US ability to control the seas around Cuba, was held to have encouraged President Kennedy in taking decisive action to get the Soviet missiles withdrawn (with a pledge by him not to invade Cuba and a secret undertaking to withdraw US nuclear missiles from Turkey).

Peter Wright, still in MI5, had done his utmost to discredit Penkovsky who, he contended, was a Soviet plant. Penkovsky, who had been under suspicion for months (as had Greville Wynne) was arrested on 22 October 1962, just before Kennedy's announcement of the 'quarantine' of Cuba and executed shortly thereafter. Greville Wynne was seized by the Russians while on a visit to Hungary but later was exchanged for a Soviet spy.

Penkovsky had a distinguished war record and important patrons within the GRU, but his father had been a White Russian officer, killed while fighting the Bolsheviks. He felt that he had been passed over for promotion. While in London, he had insisted on being dressed up in the uniforms of a British and an American colonel. He also had become fond of a bargirl called Stephanie. The KGB reaction was that this had been an extremely serious intelligence failure. As for the value of his intelligence, it included specific details about the range and other capabilities of the SS4 nuclear missiles being sent to Cuba and the revelation that, at the time, the Soviet Union had no effective first strike nuclear capability. In

1964, Khrushchev, held responsible for the Cuba misadventure, was replaced by Brezhnev.

By the 1960s, the supply of Marxist true believers in the Western intelligence agencies had dried up. Soviet agents thereafter had to be recruited with cash, while a host of Soviet and Eastern European defectors had ensured a more than equal flow of intelligence towards the West. But when it came to finding a source principled and courageous enough to provide invaluable intelligence while risking his life by staying within the Soviet system, the British struck gold with Oleg Gordievsky.

Born in 1938, he was the son of an officer in the NKVD, precursor of the KGB. A star student at the Moscow State Institute of International Relations, he studied German and the Scandinavian languages. He was a Soviet foreign service student and KGB apprentice on a course in East Berlin for six months from August 1961, during the building of the Berlin Wall. He then was trained in tradecraft and other espionage at the KGB spy school outside Moscow, before following his father and elder brother into the KGB in August 1963.

In his extraordinary and accurately titled autobiography *Next Stop Execution*, he describes how, at the risk of his life, he decided to help to undermine what he had come to regard as an evil system. His father had believed in communism as if it were a religion. The young Gordievsky started as a true believer. The first shock was when Khrushchev denounced Stalin's crimes, causing many to believe in the possibility of reforms, which then were not forthcoming. He worked zealously for the KGB on being posted to Copenhagen, but in August 1968, he was appalled by the Soviet use of force to crush the reformist movement in Czechoslovakia.

On returning to the shabbiness of Moscow, he found that 'the poison of European life' had entered his system. He missed the prosperity and openness of Danish society. In 1971, following the defection of Oleg Lyalin, the Moscow Centre was shaken by the expulsion of 105 of the KGB and GRU representatives in the Soviet Embassy in London. As three of his KGB colleagues had been expelled by the Danes, in 1972 Gordievsky was sent back to Copenhagen, under cover of becoming the Soviet Embassy's press secretary. He did his job for the KGB, cultivating the future head of the Danish Socialist People's Party as an agent, but found that all hope of reform had disappeared in the Brezhnev era.

By now, he was hoping to be contacted discreetly by the British or Americans and, encouraged to do so by the Danes, in 1974 a British intelligence officer approached him. Gordievsky insisted that he wanted no money. He was willing to help from political conviction. From the spring of 1975, a series of meetings with MI6 took place in a safe flat. British intelligence could scarcely believe their good fortune as Gordievsky was prepared to stay in place as a vital source within the KGB, a decision that he viewed as 'nothing less than undermining the Soviet system' and that he knew could cost him his life.

In 1978, he was recalled to Moscow. Contact with MI6 was suspended, as too risky. Having improved his English, he lobbied for a posting to London and was appointed there in 1982. MI6 supplied him with non-sensitive information and worked to widen his contacts, to help him to gain promotion within the KGB.

As a British agent, Gordievsky unravelled a host of mysteries for British intelligence. It was Gordievsky who finally confirmed the identity of the 'fifth' man as John Cairncross, also that the Soviet spy code named ELLI was Leo Long, recruited by Anthony Blunt. He also confirmed that the trade union leader Jack Jones had been a paid agent and identified a Labour MP who still was one. He reported that the Soviets had contacts with, but no real influence on, the Campaign for Nuclear Disarmament but contributed $1.3 million to the miners' strike. He confirmed that the KGB had no idea why Sir Roger Hollis had been investigated, as they had no relationship with him. Gordievsky enabled MI5 to trap the rogue MI5 officer Michael Bettaney into confessing. He had been passing to the Soviet London resident, Arkady Guk, all the details MI5 had about KGB and GRU operatives in Britain.

Margaret Thatcher became Gordievsky's biggest fan as she devoured his reports about Soviet intentions. These were extremely important, as he revealed the alarming extent to which the Soviets believed their own propaganda. Following Ronald Reagan's election as President, in the presence of the ailing Brezhnev, his successor Yuri Andropov had ordered the KGB and GRU to give an overriding priority to Project RYAN (an acronym in Russian for nuclear missile attack), set up to collect intelligence on the plans by the US and NATO for a surprise nuclear first strike against the Soviet Union. The KGB residencies did not believe this to be at all likely but could not afford to say so without attracting suspicion themselves.

Soviet alarmism peaked during the NATO command and control over nuclear weapons exercise ABLE ARCHER, held from 2 to 11 November 1983. Gordievsky passed to MI6 an instruction on 5 November from Moscow to the London residency warning that, once a decision was taken to launch a first nuclear strike, it could be carried out within a week to ten days. So the residency must closely observe any unusual activity in the British state institutions, including the Ministry of Defence and Downing Street, and any planned increase in blood supplies.

The British Foreign Secretary, Sir Geoffrey Howe, recorded that Gordievsky 'left us in no doubt of the extraordinary but genuine Russian fear of a real life nuclear strike.' When Robert Gates, then deputy director of the CIA, was warned of this, he was horrified. The Americans, and especially the British, attempted to reassure the Russians, including through military contacts.

Following Andropov's death in February 1984, the temperature dropped, with many Western leaders attending his funeral, including Mrs Thatcher, who, according to the Soviet Ambassador, was 'especially charming'. His successor, the also ailing Chernenko, was less paranoid about the West.

In August 1984, Mrs Thatcher expressed her concerns about Gordievsky's safety; he and his family must be protected to the full extent the UK could. In December 1984, when Chernenko's most likely successor, Mikhail Gorbachev, visited the UK in December 1984, British intelligence found itself in the unique position of writing the briefing notes for both sides – through Gordievsky for Gorbachev and direct for Mrs Thatcher, who, after their meeting, declared Gorbachev to be someone she could do business with.

To upgrade Gordievsky's position within the Soviet Embassy, the Foreign Office had expelled his line manager, Igor Titov, with Gordievsky taking over his position. Their next move was to expel the KGB resident, Arkady Guk. In April 1985, Gordievsky became the designated successor to Guk as the KGB resident in London.

MI6 shared with the CIA information from Gordievsky but, to protect him, refused to disclose their source. But Burton Gerber, the head of Soviet operations at the CIA, was determined to work out who the British source was. The task of doing so was entrusted to his colleague in counter intelligence, Aldrich Ames. They concluded that the source must be Gordievsky.

On 16 May 1985, Gordievsky suddenly was summoned back to Moscow. MI6 said that it was his decision whether to seek asylum in Britain or return to Moscow, with the obvious risk that he would be tortured or killed. But Gordievsky probably was right in feeling that, given the information he would be able to supply as the KGB resident in London, they hoped that he would return to Moscow while they updated a plan that had been developed to help to extricate him – if that proved feasible. The willingness to let him go back to Moscow yielded no further intelligence and was a potentially fatal mistake.

Neither MI6 nor Gordievsky were aware that, by then, Gordievsky had been betrayed by Aldrich Ames. It was 15 May when Ames first met and sold classified information to a KGB agent. The FBI believed that he did not explicitly identify Gordievsky until 13 June and Gordievsky himself felt that he might have been compromised in some other way. But the most probable explanation for what happened next is that Ames disclosed enough information on 15 May to trigger Gordievsky's recall and his clearer disclosure on 13 June meant that, thenceforth, Gordievsky faced an imminent risk of execution.

On returning to Moscow on 19 May, Gordievsky was drugged and interrogated for five hours by the KGB's two principal high level inquisitors. He had taken a Benzedrine pill provided by MI6 and had vowed to himself to follow Philby's rule: never confess. To the extent that he could remember what happened, he recalled at one point being told that he had confessed a few moments before (which he felt sure he hadn't), 'Now do so again.' Instead, he said that they were behaving like Stalin's prosecutors, condemning the innocent.

Having withstood the interrogation, he was told that he would never be going back to London but was not yet charged. One week after his interrogation, the London residency was told to break off contact with all the illegals, demonstrating the KGB's conviction that they had all been compromised. Gordievsky was consigned to a non operational desk job in the KGB. Under heavy surveillance and clear indications that he had been betrayed, in July he sent the planned signal to the British that he needed to be helped to escape. The Foreign Secretary, Sir Geoffrey Howe, especially, and the incoming British Ambassador, Sir Bryan Cartledge, were sceptical that the escape plan could work and feared that it would damage improving relations with the Gorbachev regime. But Margaret Thatcher was adamant that all possible efforts must be made to save Gordievsky.

So, at the second attempt, Gordievsky triggered the longstanding escape plan devised by MI6 by standing on a prearranged street corner in Moscow at 7.30 p.m. on a particular weekday, carrying a Safeway bag as a signal. An MI6 agent passed by carrying a Harrods bag and munching a Mars bar – a curiously British way of establishing contact with a secret agent in Moscow.

On 19 July, Gordievsky went for his usual jog and managed to lose his followers. He boarded a train to Vyborg near the Finnish border, then found his way to the designated wooded location where he was due to be met by two British Embassy cars driven by Raymond Asquith and Arthur Gee. But since leaving Leningrad they had Soviet police and KGB vehicles both in front and behind them. Asquith was close to despairing of losing them but, by suddenly accelerating, managed to do so just long enough to turn off the road and stuff Gordievsky into the boot of the Gees' Ford car in a mere eighty seconds, while the following cars rushed by on the other side of the trees.

In his memoir, Gordievsky describes graphically the state he was in, fearing that the rendezvous might not be made and knowing that, even if it was, if the boot of the car were opened, he faced certain execution. But with the embassy wives and children providing an element of cover and distracting the sniffer dogs, Gordievsky was smuggled through the border controls. Once safely across, having scarcely dared to believe that the rescue plan could work, Gordievsky heard within the car a full volume version of *Finlandia*. When the embassy cars stopped in Finland, Gordievsky was greeted by Veronica Price of MI6, who had devised the escape plan and ensured that it had been kept permanently ready to be activated.

For several weeks after Gordievsky's disappearance, the KGB did not know what had happened to him; it was thought that he might have committed suicide. The Russians were informed of his defection on 15 August, with no public announcement, in the vain hope that they might permit his wife and two young daughters to leave. That was not permitted for a further six years. Meanwhile, on 12 September the British announced his defection and the expulsion of twenty-five Soviet intelligence officers, triggering retaliation by the Russians against the British Embassy in Moscow. In November, in Moscow, Gordievsky was tried *in absentia* and sentenced to death.

Gordievsky's debriefing provided a further mine of information about KGB activities. In due course, he met and was thanked by both Margaret Thatcher and President Reagan and later received his award of the CMG from the Queen. Having met Leila Gordievsky, when finally she was permitted to leave Russia, I found his intrepid wife to have been coping with the ordeal she had suffered no less impressively than her husband. Sadly, however, they had been too long apart; the marriage did not survive and she and the children returned to Russia. Gordievsky, meanwhile, was continuing to provide valuable assessments about Soviet intelligence. In 1990, he cooperated with Christopher Andrew to publish *KGB: The Inside Story*.

Following his escape, on his numerous visits to Washington, Gordievsky was cordially greeted by Aldrich Ames, still a key figure in the CIA section responsible for counter-intelligence. Ames was not arrested as a Soviet spy until 1994, by which time he had been paid $4.6 million by the KGB. Having been responsible for the deaths of a number of American agents, Ames was sentenced to life imprisonment with no possibility of parole.

One of the US agents he denounced was the GRU Major General Dmitri Polyakov, who spied for the US from the 1960s to 1980. Serving in Asia, he provided valuable intelligence about the Sino-Soviet tensions. Like Gordievsky, he did so from conviction. Though he had not been active for some years, thanks to Aldrich Ames, he was executed in 1988.

So Gordievsky joined the long list of Soviet defectors to the West, having been probably the most important of all Western agents within the Soviet system. The next extraordinary source on Soviet intelligence was not a writer but the KGB archivist, Vasili Mitrokhin. When he defected to the United Kingdom in 1992, he brought with him his reconstitution of the archive of the First Chief Directorate responsible for the KGB's overseas operations in six trunks full of documents, subsequently published by him with Christopher Andrew.

Whereas in the 1930s and during the Second World War, the ideological spies had worked against the West, it was not so long thereafter that the wave of defections was overwhelmingly in the opposite direction. In a fair number of cases, above all that of Gordievsky and also of Mitrokhin, the motivation was one of principle, of disgust with the Soviet system.

In a larger number of cases, it was rather the far greater economic success of non communist countries that was the determining factor. MI5 and the FBI were right to conclude that, henceforth, the problem would be those who, like Ames and Bettaney, were motivated to become spies for money, not on any political grounds. Some of these cases were just as damaging as those, earlier, of the communist sympathisers. For decades before Gorbachev's attempts to change the system, the Soviets had been losing the battle of ideas.

The especially British fascination with tales of secret intelligence and espionage was based on a conviction, not only in the United Kingdom, that the British were pretty good at this kind of thing, especially as the Americans did not fully embrace the notion of a centralised intelligence system until after Pearl Harbour and then did so in consultation with the British, including Ian Fleming.

Ironically, the reputation for excellence in intelligence gathering in modern times did not come from agents running in the field but from signals intelligence, where the British excelled in both world wars, becoming the leaders in the computerisation of intelligence. This kind of endeavour is difficult to glamorise in print or film but increasingly eclipsed the importance of human intelligence. For, to become effective, members and the leader of organisations like the Islamic State or Al-Qaeda have to communicate with each other and Russian generals also have to communicate with their units in the field. Despite all the attempts at deception, signals intelligence (SIGINT) normally turns out to be more dependable than human intelligence (HUMINT).

After Ian Fleming, the glory days of James Bond and John le Carré, it does feel like the end of an era. But, since time immemorial, secrets have been bought and sold, by traitors, intrepid agents and shady ladies. I can see no reason why that should not continue in the future.

ACKNOWLEDGEMENTS

M y warmest thanks are due to James Stephens, Olivia Beattie and Ryan Norman of Biteback Publishing for their assistance in producing this book and to Marie-France Renwick for her help with the illustrations. My thanks also are due to the Fleming family.

LIST OF ILLUSTRATIONS

3   Sidney Reilly, the so called 'ace of spies'. © Hulton Archive / Stringer / Getty Images

4   Fidel Castro with Alec Guinness on the set of *Our Man in Havana.* © Keystone-France / Gamma-Keystone / Getty Images

5   Harold 'Kim' Philby, celebrating being 'cleared' by Harold Macmillan, 1955. © Keystone / Hulton Archive / Getty Images

6   Ian Fleming in Room 39, naval intelligence. © Spaarnestad Photo / Bridgeman Images

7   Sean Connery and Ian Fleming on the set of *Dr. No.* © Sunset Boulevard / Corbis / Getty Images

8   Ian Fleming and Ursula Andress on the set of *Dr. No.* © Bettmann / Getty Images

9   Sean Connery and Ursula Andress; handstands on the set of *Dr. No.* © Hulton Archive / Stringer / Getty Images

10 Sean Connery and Ursula Andress; handstands on the set of *Dr. No.* © United Artist / Archive Photos / Stringer / Getty Images

11 Barbara Bach on the set of *The Spy Who Loved Me.* © Sunset Boulevard / Corbis / Getty Images

12 Eva Green, *femme fatale* in *Casino Royale.* © Imago / ZUMA Press Wire

13 Alec Guinness excelling as George Smiley. © BBC Photo Archive

14 Alan Turing. © National Portrait Gallery

15 Colossus machine, Bletchley Park. © Steve Simmons / Alamy Stock Photo

16 Wrens operating the Colossus machine. © SSLP / Bletchley Park Trust / Getty Images

17 Oleg Gordievsky with President Reagan, 1987. © Eraza Collection / Alamy Stock Photo

SELECT BIBLIOGRAPHY

PRIMARY SOURCES

Christopher Andrew, with Vasili Mitrokhin, *The KGB in Europe and the West: The Mitrokhin Archive* (London: Penguin, 1999)

Christopher Andrew, with Oleg Gordievsky, *KGB: The Inside Story* (London: Hodder & Staughton, 1990)

F. M. Bailey, *A Mission to Tashkent* (Oxford: Oxford Paperbacks, 1992)

Fred Burnaby, *A Ride to Khiva* (Oxford: Oxford University Press, 2002)

Erskine Childers, *The Riddle of the Sands* (London: Penguin Classics, 2011)

Ian Fleming, *Casino Royale* (London: Vintage Classics, 2012)

Ian Fleming, *Live and Let Die* (London: Vintage Classics, 2012)

Ian Fleming, *Moonraker* (London: Vintage Classics, 2012)

Ian Fleming, *Diamonds Are Forever* (London: Vintage Classics, 2012)

Ian Fleming, *From Russia, with Love* (London: Vintage Classics, 2012)

Ian Fleming, *Dr. No* (London: Vintage Classics, 2012)

Ian Fleming, *Goldfinger* (London: Vintage Classics, 2012)

Ian Fleming, *For Your Eyes Only* (London: Vintage Classics, 2012)

Ian Fleming, *Thunderball* (London: Vintage Classics, 2012)

Ian Fleming, *The Spy Who Loved Me* (London: Vintage Classics, 2012)

Ian Fleming, *On Her Majesty's Secret Service* (London: Vintage Classics, 2012)

Ian Fleming, *You Only Live Twice* (London: Vintage Classics, 2012)

Ian Fleming, *The Man with the Golden Gun* (London: Vintage Classics, 2012)

Ian Fleming, *Octopussy and the Living Daylights* (London: Vintage Classics, 2012)

Oleg Gordievsky, *Next Stop Execution* (London: Macmillan, 1995)

Graham Greene, *The Confidential Agent* (London: William Heinemann, 1939)

Graham Greene, *The End of the Affair* (London: William Heinemann, 1951)

Graham Greene, *The Quiet American* (London: William Heinemann, 1955)

Graham Greene, *Our Man in Havana* (London: William Heinemann, 1958)

Graham Greene, *The Human Factor* (London: William Heinemann, 1978)

Graham Greene, *The Confidential Agent* (London: William Heinemann, 1939)

Bob Cullen, 'Matter of the Heart: Graham Greene's letters to his paramour, Catherine Walston, trace the hazy line between life and fiction', *Smithsonian*, June 2002

Graham Greene, Hugh Greene, *The Spy's Bedside Book* (London: Rupert Hart Davis, 1957)

Graham Greene, *A Sort of Life* (London: Bodley Head, 1971)

Peter Hopkirk, Reginald Teague-Jones (alias Ronald Sinclair), *The Spy Who Disappeared* (London: Gollancz, 1990)

Peter Hopkirk, Reginald Teague-Jones (alias Ronald Sinclair), *Diary of a Secret Mission to Russian Central Asia* (London: Gollancz, 1991)

Rudyard Kipling, *Kim* (London: Macmillan, 1901)

John le Carré, *The Spy Who Came in from the Cold* (London: Gollancz, 1963)

John le Carré, *The Looking Glass War* (London: Heinemann, 1965)

John le Carré, *A Small Town in Germany* (London: Heinemann, 1968)

John le Carré, *The Naïve and Sentimental Lover* (London: Hodder & Stoughton, 1971)

John le Carré, *Tinker Tailor Soldier Spy* (London: Hodder & Stoughton, 1974)

John le Carré, *The Honourable Schoolboy* (London: Hodder & Stoughton, 1977)

John le Carré, *Smiley's People* (London: Hodder & Stoughton, 1980)

John le Carré, *The Little Drummer Girl* (London: Hodder & Stoughton, 1983)

John le Carré, *A Perfect Spy* (London: Hodder & Stoughton, 1986)

John le Carré, *The Constant Gardener* (London: Hodder & Stoughton, 2001)

Compton Mackenzie, *Greek Memories* (London: Cassell, 1932)

Somerset Maugham, *Ashenden: Or the British Agent* (London: Heinemann, 1927)

John Milton, *The Tenure of Kings and Magistrates*, 1649

Yuri Modin, *My Five Cambridge Friends* (Toronto: Knopf, 1994)

Kim Philby, *My Silent War* (New York: Random House, 1968)

Rufina Philby, *The Private Life of Kim Philby* (London: Little, Brown, 2000)

Reginald Teague-Jones, see Peter Hopkirk

Nigel West, *The Guy Liddell Diaries, Vols I–II* (Oxford: Routledge, 2005)

Francis Younghusband, *Report of a Mission (*1897)

Francis Younghusband, *The Heart of a Continent* (New Dehli: Rupa Publications, 2000)

OTHER SOURCES

Mark Amory ed, *The Letters of Ann Fleming* (London: The Harvill Press, 1985)

Kingsley Amis, *The James Bond Dossier* (London: Jonathan Cape, 1965)

Christopher Andrew, *The Defence of the Realm: The Authorized History of MI5* (London: Allen Lane, 2009)

Christopher Andrew, *The Secret World* (London: Penguin, 2018)

Tom Bower, *The Perfect English Spy: Sir Dick White* (London: Heinemann, 1995)

Andrew Boyd, *British Naval Intelligence Through the Twentieth Century* (Barnsley: Seaforth Publishing, 2020)

Andrew Boyle, *The Riddle of Erskine Childers* (London: Hutchinson, 1977)

Andrew Boyle, *The Climate of Treason* (London: Coronet, 1987)

British Security Coordination 1940–45 (London: St Ermin's Press, 1998)

John Cooper, *The Queen's Agent* (London: Faber & Faber, 2013)

John Ferris, *Behind the Enigma* (London: Bloomsbury, 2020)

Ranulph Fiennes, *Lawrence of Arabia* (London: Penguin, 2024)

James Fleming, *Bond Behind the Iron Curtain* (London: The Book Collector, 2021)

Michael Holzman, *Spies and Traitors* (London: W&N, 2023)

Michael Holzman, *Donald and Melinda Maclean* (Chelmsford: Chelmsford Press, 2014)

Peter Hopkirk, *The Great Game* (London: John Murray, 1990)

Peter Hopkirk, *On Secret Service East of Constantinople* (London: John Murray, 1994)

Keith Jeffery, *The History of the Secret Intelligence Service* (London: Bloomsbury, 2011)

Andrew Lownie, *Stalin's Englishman* (London: Hodder & Stoughton, 2015)

Andrew Lycett, *Ian Fleming* (London: W&N, 1995)

Ben Macintyre, *007: For Your Eyes Only* (London: Bloomsbury, 2009)

Ben Macintyre, *A Spy Among Friends* (London: Bloomsbury, 2014)

Ben Macintyre, *The Spy and the Traitor* (London: Viking, 2018)

Stephen Maffeo, *Intelligence in the Age of Nelson* (Annapolis: Naval Institute Press, 2000)

Taline Ter Minassian, *Most Secret Agent of Empire* (London: Hurst, 2014)

Vasili Mitrokhin and Christopher Andrew, *The Sword and the Shield* (New York: Basic Books, 1999)

Kenneth Rose, *Elusive Rothschild* (London: Orion, 2003)

Dennis Sewell, *Cromwell's Spy* (New York: Pegasus Books, 2024)

Nicholas Shakespeare, *Ian Fleming* (London: Harvill Secker, 2023)

Ronald Sinclair, see Reginald Teague-Jones

Norman Sherry, *The Life of Graham Greene Vols 1–3* (London: Jonathan Cape, 1989, 1994, 2004)

Adam Sisman, *John le Carré* (London: Bloomsbury, 2015)

Adam Sisman, *The Secret Life of John le Carré* (London: Profile Books, 2023)

Mark Urban, *The Man Who Broke Napoleon's Codes* (London: Faber, 2001)

Rebecca West, *The Meaning of Treason* (London: Orion, 2000)

F. W. Winterbotham, *The Ultra Secret* (London: Orion, 2000)

INDEX